GRACE

BASED

DISCIPLINE

GRACE
BASED
DISCIPLINE

how to be at your best
when your kids are at their worst

Karis Kimmel Murray

family™
matters

Published by Family Matters Press, a division of Familly Matters, Inc.

Library of Congress Control Number: 2016919274

Because each individual is different and has particular physiological and
psychological needs and restrictions, the information provided in this book
does not constitute professional advice and is not a substitute for expert
medical and psychological advice.

Some names and identifying details have been changed, as well as composites
used, to protect the privacy of the individuals involved.

Author photos by Rachel Curry Photography, http://rachelcurryphotography.net

ISBN: 978-0-9827993-4-5

Printed in the United States of America

17 18 19 20 21 [VP] 6 5 4 3 2 1

For Mike, Riley, and Lydia...who give me grace.

For Mom and Dad...who named me grace.

And for Jesus...the God of grace.

contents

Acknowledgments............................IX

Foreword..................................XIII

Intro: Be at Your Best When Your Kids Are at
Their Worst.....................................1

PART ONE

1. Set an Atmosphere of Grace...................15
2. Understand Yourself and Your Kids..........29
Project: Kids Flag Page.......................45

PART TWO

3. Create Your Family Code....................53
4. Base Your Rules on God's Word.............69
Project: DIY Rule Book........................83

PART THREE

5. Evaluate Each Violation.....................91
6. Determine Your Child's Motivations.........111
7. Give Appropriate Consequences............135
8. More than Consequences...................155
Conclusion: A Clearer Picture of God.........179

APPENDICES

Four Truths for Parenting in the Digital Age....187
To Spank or Not to Spank?....................191

acknowledgements

I like to think of books as monuments. In a disposable world, a book is a lasting tribute to thousands of hours, hundreds of revisions, volumes of research, and a diverse group of heroes whose sacrifice, talent, expertise, encouragement, and skill come together to create a work that is worthy to be placed proudly on our highest hill. So here, I humbly etch these names upon my monument:

Tim and Darcy Kimmel, my good-enough, grace-based parents. What a rare and precious gift that from a very early age you told me I could write and speak powerfully. You believed I could, therefore I believed I could, and so I did. While your published works serve as the primary sources upon which *Grace Based Discipline* is built, your lives are the reason I put any stock in the words you wrote. You lived out the message of grace every day in how you loved each other and how you parented. I know that grace works because I saw it work through you.

Mike, it takes the strongest type of man to support a strong woman. Thank you for loving my crazy. Thank you for leading our family so well.

Riley and Lydia, allowing your mother the time and space to write a book is a sacrifice few can comprehend. You gave me your blessing to share difficult parts of your stories, and that takes courage. I'm proud to be your mom. At least now when you catch me making a less-than-stellar parenting decision, you can savor the irony as you quip, "*Come on,* Mom! You wrote a parenting book!"

Kory Schuknecht, when you looked me in the eye and said, "You are going to write this book," I knew that was it. Thanks for the nudge and the role you played in helping me formulate these ideas.

Sonia Cleverly, your organized mind helped craft the framework within which I could write this book. But it was your unflappable belief in me that convinced me I should.

Rustin Rossello, you prayed for me and taught me to pray.

Julie Bartolini, Michael Tooker, Edy Sutherland, Gail Schuknecht, Shaleen Kendrick, and Bill Cavness, the Dream Team of Braintrusts. Your shared experiences gave this work far greater depth than I could have alone.

Jennifer Stair, you challenged me to find my unique voice. You inspired me to orient my heart toward my readers from the very first word. You're a great editor.

Lisa Grimenstein, your sharp eye polished every line of this work.

Mary Hollingsworth, Allison Grimenstein, Kevin Harvey and the talented folks at Creative Enterprises Studio, thank you for shepherding the vital details that produce great books.

Colt, it's hard to believe that my baby brother could be an expert source in anything, but your expertise as a first responder gave me breakthrough insight into how to discipline with grace. Thank you for walking calmly toward calamity every day . . . and for fact-checking my metaphors.

Cody, thanks for being my theological sounding board. You're an okay brother too.

Shiloh, you prepared me to raise two strong-willed girls by watching our parents raise you. You're my favorite sister.

The Family Matters Board of Directors gave me a long leash and generous time to do something that none of us were sure would pan out. You are all examples of true greatness.

The Family Matters staff, especially **Jed Winkler** and **Linda DeKruyter**, for putting up with my long absences while I was writing and not begrudging the responsibility of holding down the fort. Thanks for your help, faith, and encouragement.

Trevor Palmer, is there anything you can't do? You are the epitome of chill and skill. I can't seem to create a problem that riles you, and creating problems is a talent of mine.

To all my friends, extended family, and readers who have loved me and prayed for me through this process, it's meant everything.

And finally, all my gratitude goes where all the glory belongs: always and only to the **Grace Giver.**

All is grace

Karis

One of the greatest callings in life is to be a parent. It's a chance to pour love, purpose, and hope into the human beings who typically move on to take our place. But there's an underbelly to our role as mom and dad that can sucker-punch so much of the daily joy out of this great calling.

Few things in life get us second-guessing ourselves faster than our kids' contrary behavior. In the adult world you might be known as an engaging, winsome, and otherwise successful person. But when you assume your role as a mother or father, your kids have a way of making you feel dumb as sheetrock. They also have the uncanny capacity to bring the worst out of you.

And when you do the relational math, it just doesn't seem to add up. Think about it, you're the one who consistently loves them, provides for them, protects them, and serves their myriad needs. Yet you often feel as though they don't respect your position, don't appreciate your sacrifice, have little regard for your reasonable expectations, and frequently treat you like you don't even exist.

And to that God would say, *Welcome to my world.*

God knows what you're going through. He's had to put up with these same issues when it comes to His dealings with you and me. But there are two things He doesn't do when it comes to our selfish and obstinate shenanigans. He never allows them to have any influence over His commitment to consistently love us. And He doesn't react to them; He responds. And He does it graciously.

In fact, His grace shows up most when we're hardest to love and clearly in need of an outside-in course correction in behavior.

It's ironic when you consider this against the backdrop of how grace is so often misrepresented. Too many people think grace is just human kindness on Red Bull. They assume that grace and discipline are opposites. But God's treatment of you and me tells a very different story. God disciplines us, and His discipline is a tangible form of grace. It's a grace that communicates that His love is never passive but rather rolls up its sleeves to guide and shape us toward behavior and choices that are in our best interest.

Years ago, I wrote the book *Grace Based Parenting* to help moms and dads see what God's grace looks like lived out in highs and lows of family dynamics. Since then, the number one request has been for a follow-up book that unpacks what God's grace looks like when it comes to disciplining our kids. I always felt there was someone better qualified to write that book, someone who had been on the receiving end of discipline administered within an atmosphere of God's grace all through their childhood.

You see, when my wife, Darcy, and I became parents, we decided we would treat our kids the way God treats us, and that's with grace. Obviously we're flawed people. And we made our fair share of missteps along the way. But God's grace proved to be sufficient in more ways than we could have ever imagined. His grace especially came to our rescue when it came time to deal with our kids' unacceptable behavior.

This book is written by one of those kids. It's the words of a girl who was not only an honor to raise, but who's been an inspiration to watch take on adult life. Karis was born with a huge capacity to put a whole lot into any given moment. She's equally gifted with the ability to pull a whole lot out as well. While she wasn't a particularly hard child to raise, she wasn't exactly an easy one either. Her tireless antics often left us feeling exhausted. I can't count how many times I said, "She did what?!?" into the receiver when my wife would call to relay the events of the day.

There were many nights when I stood at the door of her bedroom and watched her slip off to sleep after a day of putting our patience on life support. And as I stood there I'd pray, *Oh Lord, please don't let us mess up this wonderful child.*

Karis is rounding the bend on two decades as a wife and mother. She lives life with her feet joyfully sloshing around in the goo of reality while her heart spills over with the grace God used to save her soul. It's been fun to watch her and Mike raise their kids. They understand what grace-based discipline looks like—discipline that is guided by God's truth and tempered by His grace. She and Mike were assigned two girls who were hardwired to know how to give them a run for their money. Yet, they've found God's grace to be more than adequate when it comes to navigating their girls through the nuances of self-focused childhood.

I'm sure I'm biased, but I think you're really going to enjoy the way Karis says what she says. This girl has had a way with words since the day words first started coming out of her mouth. But more importantly, I know you're going to be far more effective as a parent because of the case she builds for God's grace leading the way in the grittier areas of your relationship with your kids. When it comes to disciplining your kids, God's grace is the game-changer.

With all of this said, it's an honor to introduce to you Karis Kimmel Murray and her book *Grace Based Discipline*.

Dr. Tim Kimmel

BE AT YOUR BEST WHEN YOUR KIDS ARE AT THEIR WORST

Did you know that firefighters never run into a burning building? I wouldn't have realized that, except my brother Colt is a firefighter.

This is what he told me: Everyone else tries to run if they can. Those who are inside the burning building try to run out. Those who have a loved one inside try to run in. Bystanders, choking on the smoke, run away. But a firefighter walks. Resolutely. Briskly, perhaps, but calmly. With every step he carefully assesses the situation so he can respond effectively.

Running into a fire would get a firefighter's blood pumping and elevate his heart rate. He can't waste precious oxygen in the tank he carries. He knows the lives of the people inside the inferno that he's walking toward depend on him showing up calm and well equipped to face the flames.

Firefighters, paramedics, police officers, ER doctors and nurses—we call them "first responders" for a reason. While most people *react* to a crisis situation with a volatile cocktail of fear, panic, and white knuckles, these men and women know their role is to meet danger and disaster with the appropriate response.

In a sense, parents are also first responders. We may not have realized we volunteered, but that's the position we often find ourselves in.

For example, once when my older daughter was two and my younger one was about six months, we took a fateful trip to Walmart. It was the first time I'd been out of the house with both girls in five weeks. We'd had more than a month of back-to-back viruses, ear infections, and various gastrointestinal crises.

We'd reached the point on Oregon Trail where a bleak line of text rolls across the computer screen to announce: YOU HAVE DIED OF DYSENTERY.

Also, we were out of supplies. Taking a toddler and a baby on a giant supply haul to Walmart is no one's idea of fun. Kids have a tolerance fuse for shopping trips, and it's often lit before you even back down your driveway.

We needed everything: food, diapers, formula, toilet paper, milk, printer toner, shampoo. I was racing my double-wide cart through every section of the store, trapped in my own manic episode of *Supermarket Sweep*, trying to get all the items on my list before two little bombs exploded.

I would've made it if my flip-flop hadn't snapped. And I would have ignored it and walked out with only one shoe, except it was July in Phoenix. The air was 115 degrees. The surface of the parking lot's asphalt was approximately eleven-thousand degrees.

"Mommy needs just *one more thing*, girls," I offered, as I imagine doomed sailors might dump gold overboard to appease the Kraken.

I hobbled, pushing my load to the shoe department where I'd resolved to grab the first pair of flip-flops I saw. When we got there, I had a moment of weakness and agreed to let Riley, my toddler, out of the blessed confinement of the cart's buckled child seat.

She was free! She looked at me, and I saw a flash of savage bloodlust in her eyes. She squared her little shoulders at the end of a corridor of footwear, put out both her arms at opposite sides of the shoebox-lined shelves, and walked resolutely to the end—knocking off all the boxes like giant dominoes.

Her fuse had run out, and now the Walmart shoe department looked like a bomb had gone off. Fellow shoppers stared as the shrapnel of laces, sandals, cardboard, and my pride settled into smoke and rubble. It was a miracle that I didn't leave my kids in the endcap of aisle 9 with *Rollback $4.97* price tags taped to their little foreheads.

That day I had to act as a first responder, whether I liked it or not. Since then, I've had many more days like it, and I'm sure you have too.

Our kids have a way of igniting our plans, standards, and expectations and then burning them to the ground. Whether the accelerant they use is immaturity, peer pressure, or blatant dis-obdience, the end result is the same: a crime scene.

Our kids like to mess with us. That's how it feels, at least. This is real life. These kids we're raising didn't come with an instruction manual. Ideally, we're supposed to respond to their disobedience, rebellion, and immaturity like a cop calmly making a routine traffic stop. Only, we often feel a whole lot more like the hostage who is bound and gagged in our kids' trunk.

Our standard default mode is to freak out. And that's exactly what we'll do unless we are prepared to do something different.

It's tough to respond rather than react when you feel like, and sometimes *are*, the victim of your kids' behavior. Yet God (the Ultimate Parent) tells us how He responds to His children's behavior: with grace-based discipline. And He also tells us why: "The Lord disciplines the one he loves" (Hebrews 12:6). In this book, I will show you how to use grace-based discipline to respond to your kids the way God responds to us.

Just Tell Me What I'm Supposed to Do with These Kids!

Chances are, you picked up this book because you have kids and are trying to figure out how to get them to do what you say. If this describes you, weary parent, then I know how you feel. Never in your wildest dreams did you think a three-year-old could bring you to your knees, but that's where you find yourself as you tell them for the thirtieth time to stop pushing the buttons on the TV. And who could have known how exhausting it is to have a twelve-year-old critique every request you make of them? If you're like me, you're pretty sure that any day now everyone will discover that you have no clue what you're doing. When you brought your little love bundle home from the hospital or adoption agency, you might have been prepared for sleepless nights, diaper changes, and constant demands. But about the time you first stared into your new child's eyes, you got throat-punched by the responsibility of guiding that love bundle from the pack 'n play all the way to adulthood. You find yourself asking essential questions like, "How did my tiny three-year-old fit nine raisins in his left nostril?" "Where did she even find that purple Sharpie?" "Why can't they ever just do what I ask?"

I *get* it.

Those overwhelming feelings of uncertainty, fear, insufficiency, and exhaustion? I try to keep them shut up, too, but they nag. They vibrate across my mind and whisper that I'm not enough.

If you have toddlers or preschool-aged children, I'm just ten minutes up the road. If you have tweens and teens, we're walking hip to hip. I can give you a heads-up about some loose gravel you'll likely encounter as we take each holy step along this dusty road of parenthood and grace-based discipline. If we get lost, we can whisper a frantic prayer together.

Before I had kids, I thought I had this discipline thing on *lock*. I mean, my parents literally wrote the book on parenting. (More on that in a bit.) Not only did I hear my parents teach about grace-based parenting my whole life, but my siblings and I were parented that way in our real, everyday lives. By the time I was a young adult, I was convinced that I knew everything there was to know about how to be a parent.

Then I became one. I came to realize that kids are born with a free will. Turns out, discipline is not as easy as simply telling kids *no*. Who would have thought?

We all know we need to discipline our kids. I mean, we hear it everywhere—from friends, the media, our parents, and parenting experts. But as we walk the daily road of discipline and try to make the right decisions for our kids, the actual process of discipline gets convoluted.

We just want the 140-character version of what we should do and what we should say when our kids' behavior scrapes the enamel off our sanity.

Good-Bye, Best-Laid Plans

My husband and I got hitched when I was twenty and he was twenty-two. We had a five-year life plan: we would finish college, then Mike would launch a business while I wrote for a newspaper, and then, maybe, we'd start a family. But in less than a year, our five-year plan went off the rails. As I was pursuing my B.A. in journalism from Arizona State University, we ended up with a B.A.B.Y. instead. When our first daughter was eleven months old, my husband and I learned I was expecting again! New life plan: just whatever.

By my twenty-third birthday I was a haphazard and, at times, reluctant mother of two girls. I mean, in my Millennial generation, twenty-three-year-olds were expected to go to grad school and brunch. I was enrolled in mommy boot camp and couldn't even remember the last time I'd eaten warm food. While the men and women in my graduating class were writing doctoral dissertations, interning at Corporate Ladder Inc., or cutting their teeth in full-time Christian ministry, I was reading *Good Night Moon*, climbing the ladder at the playground, and ministering to two little screaming creatures who were *actually* cutting their teeth! My résumé is written in crayon and stained with drool.

The First to Yell, "Geronimo!"

Yet I do have one unique qualification that might incline you to listen to me when it comes to parenting and discipline.

I'm the wind dummy.

It's a technical term. In parajumping, particularly in military settings, the wind dummy is an object that is the average size, shape, and weight of the soldiers who plan to jump from the aircraft. And, in case you haven't guessed, the wind dummy is thrown from the plane in unpredictable or untested jumping situations to help soldiers see where they will land and whether or not the jump is safe.

So remember how I told you that my dad wrote the book on parenting? He is a well-known Christian author and speaker, and I was his wind dummy. As the oldest of his four children, all of his revolutionary parenting theories were first tested on—you guessed it—*me*.

For you to understand where I'm coming from as a parent, first let me tell you a bit about my own parents.

There Has to Be a Better Way

In the early 1980s, my mom and dad knew that if the God of the universe called them to be parents, then He must have a plan to equip them for this vital role. Yet, at the time, no one had established a comprehensive theology of parenting. Sure, there was a smattering of spiritual guidance and advice from pastors and Christian authors, but there was no tested, holistic, biblical plan for parenting. To my mom and dad, becoming parents felt like jumping blindly from an airplane.

They never set out to change the landscape of Christian parenting. They had no visions of writing books or speaking to arenas full of parents. They only knew that they weren't willing to make their skydive into parenting wearing the existing, defective parachutes of fear, sin management, or spiritual image control.

They knew God's Word held a bigger picture, and they begged God to reveal it to them.

Finding Grace

The epiphany smacked my mom across the forehead when she read Matthew 23:9, in which Jesus says, "Call no man your father on earth, for you have one Father, who is in heaven." She shared what she'd discovered with my dad, and together they formulated a revolutionary hypothesis: since God is our heavenly Father and we are His children, we have a parenting model to follow that is a story woven into the whole Scripture. Their theory illuminated every interaction between God and humans and allowed them to see those interactions for what they really were: parenting!

Through this lens, they could see that our Father did not base His relationship with His kids on behavior modification, fear, or retaliation. Our holy heavenly Father's loving relationship with His sinful children is based on only one thing: His decision to extend grace, *undeserved favor*, in order to have a relationship with us.

That's when my mom and dad became convinced that the theology of parenting is simply this: treat the people you are called to love the way God treats you—with grace.

It's the Landing That Counts

My mom and dad began encouraging parents to abandon the moralistic, fear-based parachutes they'd been using and strap on grace instead. Not surprisingly, many were reluctant. My parents could talk all they wanted about how their biblical "calculations" of grace-based parenting looked promising, but ultimately, they had to throw a wind dummy out of the plane and see where it would land.

That dummy was me. I'm the oldest of their four children, and our family was the proving ground for grace-based parenting.

I assure you that my parents tested their hypothesis with compassionate conviction. They were so committed to the idea that the theology of parenting was grounded in God's grace that they were willing to use those principles on their own children. And, as He so often does, God proved we can trust His example as the Ultimate Parent.

The Jump Data

My three siblings and I, along with so many other children raised with grace-based parenting, have landed safely into adulthood. The jump, while it wasn't without strong and turbulent winds, confirms that God's grace is the ever-reliable parachute to which we can trust our lives.

My mom and dad, Dr. Tim and Darcy Kimmel, founded Family Matters out of the core belief that God's grace can encourage, educate, and equip families for every age and stage of life. Their internationally hosted parenting and marriage events, radio and television broadcasts, articles, videos, website, and best-selling books, especially *Grace Based Parenting* and *Grace Filled Marriage*, have been used by God to transform tens of thousands of families into instruments of His restoration and reformation. And I am honored to be part of the Family Matters ministry team alongside them.

In this book, I will answer the most frequently asked questions our ministry receives: "When my daughter hauls off and _____, and when my son yells _____, *what should I do?*" Fill that first blank with the most annoying, undesirable, infuriating verb in your kids' repertoire. Fill that second blank with the most disrespectful, dishonest, unrighteous phrase you've heard escape your kids' mouths. It'll be like a delinquent version of Mad Libs. We've heard it all.

Parents are asking the same basic question: "How do I discipline my kids?" The problem is, there's no singular answer.

But there are answers. We'll look at some.

Respond—Don't React

Parents face a crazy paradox. We love our kids exactly as they are, *but we also love them too much to let them stay that way.* That's why it's vital that we learn how to put aside our emotional reactions long enough to respond to our children when they need discipline, especially when we are the victims of their behavioral crime spree.

In order to get control of our emotional reactions so that we can respond instead, we must take two counterintuitive action steps:

- Choose not to take their behavior personally, even if it is.
- Don't waste your emotional oxygen huffing and puffing about your kids' behavior.

The Bible reminds us that we gave birth to sinners (Romans 3:23). We shouldn't be surprised when they act that way.

Put It in the Basket

The vital action steps above are easier said than done. In order to treat our kids the way God treats us, we've got to see our kids the way God sees us. Fortunately, my parents shared an important principle with me about how they were able do that: *You must separate your child's behavior from their heart.*

As parents, we love our kids' hearts, but we don't always love their behavior. So let me teach you a mental exercise that I use to separate the two.

I like to imagine a basket. Anytime one of my kids does or says something that I consider bad behavior, I imagine myself scooping up that behavior and putting it in the basket. Like cleaning up debris, I mentally gather up the carnage of my kid's conduct and place it in my basket. Then I walk the imaginary basket into another room and place it on a shelf. Now when I come back and look at my child, I'm a lot more likely to see her potential instead of her problems, her character rather than her corruption. I'm able to glimpse, if even incompletely, the heart that God sees when He looks at her.

God sees us (His children) in light of Christ's atonement and forgiveness. He sees us through the filter of grace and mercy. Our heavenly Father still disciplines our behavior (because that's what a loving parent does), but He chooses not to define us by it.

Now, I'm not suggesting that the actions, words, and choices that we put in the basket have no consequences. Everything has earthly consequences. We'll talk in part 3 about what to do with the bothersome behaviors you put in the basket—but first, we have to separate the behavior from our child so we can really see his or her heart.

In my own life, this mental exercise has been instrumental to disciplining with grace. When I practice this exercise, remarkable things start to happen. Nothing about the situation has really changed, but suddenly, I'm able to see my daughter's heart more clearly. I'm able to calmly gather up the wreckage of a shoe aisle tantrum and see a heart that needs me, her mom, to love her even while she's exploding.

This mental exercise has been a powerful tool for me, and it can be for you, too, because:

- It doesn't require permission or cooperation from our kids (or anyone else for that matter).
- It enables us to defuse our emotions, rather than allowing them to drive us.
- It provides the opportunity to love our kids as God loves them.
- It allows us to define our kids by who they are, not what they do.
- It empowers us to discipline our kids, not from a place of hurt, fear, or retaliation, but from a place of love that has their best interests in mind.

Grace-Based Parenting Requires Responding, Not Reacting

My husband and I were both raised with grace, so we arrived at parenting with a high relational net worth. Yet, we've still had to learn how to respond, rather than react, to our kids. It doesn't come naturally to even the most well-prepared parents.

We've had to choose, over and over again, to parent and discipline our kids the way God parents and disciplines us. The grace-based approach to relationships works, but it's not a method; it's a paradigm. And if grace is not your current context, shifting away from whatever broken relationship model you've adopted or inherited from your family of origin takes time.

Disciplining our kids with grace requires us to parent like first responders. But the good news is, becoming a responsive parent doesn't require you to have superpowers or know how to parse Greek verbs. I know this because I don't and I can't. Grace-based, responsive parents aren't born; they're *made*. We're just ordinary people tapping into extraordinary help. If you're willing to let Him, God can teach you to respond to your children by walking confidently toward, rather than running terrified from, the burning building that is your kids' behavior.

In this book I will put some handles on how the grace-based philosophy applies specifically to discipline, so you can get a firm grip on it and put it to practical use the next time your kids.

Actually, you might want to go check on them. It's been quiet too long. Silence is golden, unless you have a three-year-old. Then it's trouble!

PART ONE

BUILDING HEALTHY RELATIONSHIPS

Rules without relationships lead to rebellion.
–Josh McDowell

chapter one

SET AN ATMOSPHERE OF GRACE

Do not be overrighteous, neither be overwise—why destroy yourself? Do not be overwicked, and do not be a fool— why die before your time? It is good to grasp the one and not let go of the other. Whoever fears God will avoid all extremes.
— Ecclesiastes 7:16–18 NIV

We'd moved in to our new home a week prior. Between Mike and me, my parents, my sister, my best friend, and an acquaintance who was a talented interior designer, we'd repainted, unpacked, organized, installed new window treatments, and hung every piece of art and photo in its place.

It was my dream house. We came to view it an hour after it came on the market. We started walking through the backyard first. Before we even reached the back porch, we told our Realtor to go out to his car and write the contract.

Didn't we want to look inside? he asked. No, we said. If it had walls, floors, plumbing, and at least one working toilet inside, that would be enough. We'd buy it. The resort backyard would make living in a shanty worth it.

But the interior was delightful and well maintained. It was as if someone had found our list of everything we were looking for in a house, even the ridiculous criteria like a front courtyard with a raised bed for herbs and an electrical outlet in the floor centered in front of the picture window so we wouldn't have to run an extension cord to plug in our Christmas tree.

It even had a chicken coop! And it wasn't some functional, ugly thing. It was the cottage you might stumble upon in the poultry version of *Snow White*. To top it off, the seller asked if we'd like to keep the heritage hens who inhabited it. She was moving to a town where she couldn't take Nugget, Noodle, Dumpling, and Coco with her. One of them even laid green eggs. Hand on the Bible, I've wanted a coop of backyard hens, with at least one who lays green eggs, since I was a girl and read the Little House on the Prairie books.

We had planned for this for so long. The house hit all the marks. Our friends and family had helped us get it completely ready, down to the last bathroom drawer, for the open house we'd foolishly planned for today, exactly seven days after moving in. Yeah, it was crazy, but we just couldn't wait to share our new home with our friends and neighbors.

Everything was perfect, but we had to cancel the open house at the last minute. All day we'd tried our best to manage, but finally we packed a few bags and headed to the Holiday Inn for the night.

Atmosphere Is Everything

It was late April.

We'd planned our move and open house at a time of year in Phoenix when you occasionally need to run your heat, but you definitely don't need your air conditioner. Well, you *shouldn't* need it. Unless you get a freak one-hundred-degree day when it should be in the mid-seventies.

Okay, we thought. *We'll just keep the guests inside and let the brave ones venture out to see the backyard hens while the rest of us stay in the climate-controlled house and drink iced tea.*

We turned on our AC unit, the one we'd just had inspected prior to closing, and heard it come to life. It ran for hours, but the temperature never cooled. We checked the coolant, restarted the fan, changed the filters, and did everything else we could think of. The repairman couldn't come till Monday. We tried to convince ourselves that we, and perhaps even our most loyal friends, could still power through and have our open house. But it was miserable. The chickens were laying hard-boiled eggs, for the love.

You know the feeling. If you're too hot or too cold, it's hard to think about anything else, much less enjoy even the most perfect, otherwise comfortable house. Forget triple digits, a home that's even a few degrees over or under a comfortable temperature nags at the people inside and creates a low-grade uneasiness that sucks the rest and joy right out of them.

The Temperature of Grace

Grace is like the perfect temperature. It's that sweet-spot equilibrium of truth and mercy in which we thrive. As parents, we can plan, prepare for, and try to do everything right yet still get an outcome we don't expect or intend. If the climate of our home falls on either side of grace, it can completely undermine our methods, even if those methods are correct and well-intended.

When the repairman finally came, he diagnosed our problem as a faulty thermostat. The air-conditioning unit was running— all systems were go—but because our malfunctioning thermostat wasn't giving the air-conditioning unit an accurate temperature reading, it could not successfully control the temperature inside the house.

A broken spiritual thermostat can cause our homes to reach extreme temperatures—too hot or too cold, depending on the outside environment. Let's identify and define the extremes:

- *Legalism*—Toxic hyperfocus on the rules, standards, and law that is motivated by a believer's lack of acceptance that salvation is a gift not a debt; an unbelief that God's grace alone is what saved them. (Romans 3:21–26)
- *License*—Toxic negligence of the rules, standards, and law that is motivated by a believer's lack of acceptance that salvation must progress toward holiness; an unbelief that God's grace alone should change them. (Romans 12:1–2)

Legalistic parents create a scorching atmosphere that dictates behavior modification and sin management in order to "earn" God's favor, which leaves their kids burned by contaminated religion and crippling shame. At the other extreme, license-based parents create a frigid atmosphere that ignores the implications that God's commandments have on their behavior, which leaves their kids frozen by spiritual chaos and painful consequences.

Jesus went to the cross to forever free us and to help us overcome the unbelief that often leads us toward these extremes.

We can't fix what we don't know is broken, so identifying our broken thermostats is the first step to allowing God to fix them and bring extreme temperatures back into balance.

We need God's help to ensure that the climate of our homes is grace. In our own power, our thermostats will constantly malfunction because of our own sin nature.

Before I unpack the strategies of effective, grace-based discipline, it's important that we check our home's thermostat. Really, everything hinges on this. We can follow a checklist perfectly, but if we miss grace . . . well, it makes for an uncomfortable journey for everyone involved. And since we know that we are imperfect human parents raising imperfect human kids, we all need the thermostat set on grace even more.

Want to hear some good news? Grace-based homes are places where good outcomes and strong, lasting relationships don't rise or fall based on our ability to follow a protocol. And God continues to give us grace, even when our shoddy thermostats threaten to ruin the party.

What Is Grace?

Grace is God's unmerited favor. God offers us His favor not because of what we deserve or because of who we are, but because of who He is. In spite of us, He loves us and wants to have a loving relationship with us, but our sin is in the way. So Christ's death on the cross paid for all of our sin, all our failings—past, present, and future—and created a way for us to receive grace and salvation. Because of Jesus, we have a pathway to experience the favor God wants to give us and the loving relationship He wants to have with us. God's grace adopts us into His family and gives us a new identity as His sons and daughters.

The grace that brings about this new identity has everything to do with God's character and nothing to do with us. We don't compel God to offer us His grace; He does it out of love. Since we didn't do anything to cause God to give us our new identity, then there's nothing we can do to cause Him to withdraw it. And it's impossible to do anything to gain *more identity and favor* because we already have it! There are no levels of identity. When we repent of our sin and accept God's love and forgiveness, His grace declares once and for all that we are His. The end.

That's how God parents us, and that's why a grace-based home is one where our kids know that their identity as a loved member of our family doesn't hinge on their behavior.

God's grace doesn't mean that His rules, boundaries, and standards disappear. God expects for His sons and daughters to obey Him. Even while we're enjoying a loving, grace-based relationship with our heavenly Father, the Bible makes it clear that the lines are still drawn, crossing them is still sin, and there are still consequences. Our behavior has no effect on God's love for us, but it does affect how we perceive and experience our relationship with our loving Father. Sinful choices rob us of our ability to feel the full measure of joy that God intends for us.

In the same way, a grace-based home isn't one where rules, boundaries, and standards don't exist. Our kids need consequences for their choices and behavior, but they need to feel sure that our love and grace for them will remain steady and constant regardless.

You Don't Have to Be Perfect

More than ever, my generation of parents is strapped with the oppression of perfectionism when it comes to raising our kids. It's a poison pill that society has dealt us and we have freely swallowed.

One thing my dad taught me about parenting is this: You don't have to be a perfect parent; you already aren't. You just have to be a good-enough, grace-based parent.

You also don't have to be perfect in how you discipline your kids. You don't have to do and say all the perfect things when your kids' behavior requires discipline. You just need to be *good enough* at disciplining your kids with grace.

There are no perfect first responders. They might seem super-human, but they're still fully mortal, fallible, and vulnerable. Yet, they intentionally orient themselves toward a crisis situation and try to respond *as best they can*. If you can learn to be like them, *even just some of the time*; if you can halt your emotional, fear-based reactions to your kids' behavior and convert that effort into a deliberate (albeit imperfect) response instead, *even if it's only one time in ten*, you'll already be light-years ahead of the reactionary, perfectionism-strapped parents that so many of us are by default. And with each conscious, *good-enough* response, rather than unconscious reaction, your kids reap the benefits.

Grace in Action

My life is full of examples of times my parents and friends responded to my misbehaviors and mistakes with grace. I remember one huge mistake that ended up being a great showcase of grace in action.

I had outpatient surgery scheduled for the day before my oldest daughter Riley's first birthday to fix an issue that giving birth to her had caused. Women's bodies never look the same post-children, and they never function the same either. *(All God's ladies said amen.)*

I hadn't planned to do a party for Riley on her exact birthday because I didn't know how I would feel post-surgery. Since it was an outpatient procedure and I'd recover at home, I thought it wouldn't be wise to push myself. After all, I'd found that typically a doctor's definition of "slight discomfort" differs wildly from everyone else's.

I figured I'd give myself a few weeks and then throw the most epic thirteen-month birthday party my friends had ever seen. Bouncy houses and chocolate fountains for days!

The surgeon sent me home with the lingering effects of anesthesia and a prescription. Rest and narcotics were the only things on my agenda for at least a week.

The next day was Saturday, Riley's first birthday. Mike had taken her with him on some errands so I could sleep since I was only about twenty hours post-surgery. The phone rang on the coffee table next to me. I answered and heard my sister-in-law Sara's voice on the other end of the line.

"Do you want me to pick up anything for the party today?"

"What?" I was still hazy-headed from my medications. I couldn't decode her words.

Sara asked again, "Can I bring anything?"

"Um, what?" I said again. "Can you bring anything to *what?*"

"To the party. To Riley's birthday party." Sara was speaking in a slow, concerned meter. "You called yesterday and invited us to come to a birthday party for Riley today."

Long pause. There was a battle between lucidity and pharmaceuticals raging in my mind. Puzzle pieces of memories were trying to fill in the last twenty-four hours.

Sara didn't know about my surgery. She was eight months pregnant, and I hadn't wanted her to fuss over me.

"It was weird," she said. "You kept saying, 'It's important . . . It's tomorrow.' You sounded asleep. In fact, you sound like you're sleeping now!"

"I had surgery yesterday."

"What? What the heck are you doing having a party today! Are you crazy?"

Tears and the crackers I'd eaten that morning were surfacing. I was trying hard to suppress them both. I must've been harboring serious subconscious guilt for postponing Riley's first birthday party. It was coming back. I was remembering.

"I may have called a few people."

But, Lord, mercy! How many people?

I thought that this must be what it was like to wake up

hungover, trying to piece together the events of a wild night. I saw about twenty Rolodex[1] cards littering the end table by the sofa I was sprawled on.

I took a frantic inventory of the loose Rolodex cards. I explained to Sara what I must've done and started reading off the names over the phone: half a dozen playgroup moms, several ladies from Bible study, and three neighbors, including the bachelor across the street! That wasn't counting anyone I'd called whose numbers I'd memorized.

"What time did I say the party was?"

Sara had a loosely veiled laugh in her voice. "Who starts a party at 11:45 a.m.? Such a strangely specific time . . ."

Someone on drugs, that's who. I looked at the clock. It was 10:27.

"Oh my gosh, Sara! Can you come early!?"

"Sure." She said they'd leave their house in ten minutes.

"Bring ice!" I instructed before frantically hanging up.

I felt nauseous at the reality of what was about to happen. An unknown number of people were about to arrive at my house for a party I'd apparently planned while drugged.

I called my husband, who was at the hardware store with Riley, and screamed, "Come home now!"

The next call was to my parents' house. Dad was out of town, but Mom had stayed to help with Riley during my surgery and recovery. I quipped that maybe she should have been babysitting me instead. I told her what I'd done, and Mom said she and my brother would hurry over ASAP.

---

1 It was 2003. A Rolodex was what we did before we could store contacts in our smartphones.

I dragged my groggy body off the couch, brushed my teeth and hair, changed out of my pajamas, put on lipstick and deodorant, and pinched my cheeks.

Then I dumped the dirty clothes out of a laundry basket onto my bed, rushed back out to the living room with the basket, and gathered used tissues, partially eaten saltines, the Rolodex, and the now-dying cordless[2] phone. Then I headed for the kitchen, threw all the dirty dishes in the basket, and shoved it behind the laundry room door.

I frantically wiped down the counters, found two pizzas in my freezer (the boxes did say "party pizzas"), and dug through my pantry for a cake mix I'd bought a few months before. I didn't have any icing.

My mom and brother and Mike and Riley, swarmed into the house at the same time. I was frantically cutting Totino's pizza into fancy squares and arranging it on the only two clean plates in the house. I realized I was about to burn the cupcakes and yanked them out of the oven.

Mom put Riley in a clean dress, and my brother swept the porch.

Mike called his parents. Who knows what he told them.

As my sister-in-law and brother-in-law charged through the door (with ice I had no beverages for), I was tearing paper towels off a roll to use as napkins.

Sara found some powdered lemonade and paper cups in my cupboard and started letting the other guests in as they arrived promptly.

At 11:45 a.m.

---

2 Circa 2003, the cordless phone was the wall phone's cooler, hipper cousin. See also: landlines.

I said a blurry thank-you to the (twelve!) guests as they saun-
tered, bewildered, into the living room. And yes, one of them was
my bachelor neighbor, bless him. Several guests brought gifts for
Riley.

Exhausted and still significantly drugged, I motioned toward
the pizza and lemonade on the coffee table, laid back down on
the couch, and slept through most of the party.

Percocet Made Calamity;
Community Made Good

I have only one photo from Riley's first birthday party. She's
sitting in her highchair, a bow from one of her presents stuck to
her bald head, reaching toward a lit match someone stuck in an
icing-less cupcake.

I'd made a train wreck of a day that was supposed to be a
milestone. Maybe a few people decided to come at such short notice for the same reason we watch cringe-worthy reality TV. But,
mostly, my friends and family came to the train-wreck party and
made the best of frozen pizza, lemonade, and dry cupcakes for
a more noble reason: compassion. They gave my daughter gifts,
smiled through the birthday song, and tucked me into bed on
their way out.

I'd bent all the rules of good hospitality. I'd violated every code
of party etiquette. I'd earned social humiliation . . .

. . . but that's not what I got.

Redeeming the Wreckage

I'm fortunate to have people in my life who have experienced
and extend to others the grace of God. They see relationships
on a parallel plane with rules and believe tolerance is as vital as

etiquette. In their own way, those friends, family, and acquaintances showed me love and grace that day. They redeemed the wreckage of my drug-dial party planning.

Who knows what would've happened if Sara hadn't called? She's since told me that she just felt a nudge—that my phoned-in, sleepy-sounding birthday invite had seemed too *off*. She, my mom, my brother, and my brother-in-law all came to my rescue. And Mike, if he felt any, did not show one stitch of embarrassment on my behalf.

It's a funny story . . . now. And, truly, it's a trivial thing in the grand scheme. But it could've become a big thing, at least to me. I put a high value on my friends and neighbors and a huge premium on hospitality. I'm a highly social extrovert. My people are my life. If my guests had focused only on the broken rules and fumbled etiquette and had given no consideration to the context surrounding my pharmaceutically impaired behavior, that day could have been a huge source of shame for me. But instead, the potential damage was tempered, all around, by our relationships.

Instead, I remember it as a day defined by grace.

Good Discipline Is Always for Our Kids

We encounter fork-in-the-road opportunities in our homes all the time. Our kids are going to break rules, big and small. They will skirt etiquette and cross boundaries. We have the choice to turn these times toward shame or joy. Because we are human, we won't always get it right. But we know from watching our heavenly Father parent His children that grace means responding with discipline in a way that is *for* our kids. It's the force of love applied for them, rather than against them. The point of discipline is not retaliation, but to act in our kids' best interests. Discipline, when done right, is for our kids' ultimate good.

If our homes are defined by rules at the expense of relationships, our kids will rebel against us. On the flip side, if we ignore the rules, our relationships are undermined and our kids will end up resenting us.

The only way any of us finds the right temperature in our homes is to remember that grace flows freely from our loving Father. We can take the grace that saved us into the rest of our lives and let it empower us as parents. Our Father loves us, He forgives us for our inadequacies, and He will replace our broken thermostats with His as many times as we need it.

When Mercy Is Right

Usually grace-based discipline requires enforcing, or at least allowing, uncomfortable consequences to shape our kids' character and teach them they must live by God's standards. Sometimes it requires squashing their small bratty behaviors now so they don't grow into big bratty behaviors later.

Grace refuses to allow our kids to grow up to be jerks in a world that doesn't suffer fools. Rules are important! When our kids thumb their noses at the rules, sometimes grace looks a lot like standing on their air hoses until we get their full cooperation.

Yet sometimes grace looks like redeeming their mistakes and absorbing their consequences. That's what my family and friends did for me on Riley's birthday. They sprang into action to reboot what should've been a disaster.

Sometimes the shame and regret our kids already feel as a result of their behavior *is* the consequence . . . and it's enough. In those times we can stand as their shield. That doesn't mean we don't acknowledge what they did or that we'll be able to erase all the damage, especially if it's serious. And it doesn't mean we toss out the rulebook. But there are times when it's appropriate to choose mercy for our kids.

Because we talk so much of grace, it's important to note that mercy, at least for our purposes in this book, has a distinct definition from grace. Mercy means we *do not* receive the penalty we deserve for what we did. Grace means we *do* receive God's favor and love regardless of our behavior. None of us deserves even one second of God's concern or attention, but because He loves us, He gives it anyway. Because we are all undeserving, any attention paid to us by God is therefore a form of grace, discipline included.

So, having a grace-based relationship with our kids simply means they have our favor and love regardless. They keep their identity as our loved sons and daughters no matter what. But that love often requires that we discipline them, and discipline is a spectrum of responses, from mercy to heavy consequences, all of which are forms of grace when they are done with our kids' best interest as our ultimate goal.

The only way we'll be able to discern whether to give our children consequences, mercy, or anything in between is if we've built a close enough relationship with our kids to afford us some perspective. That's the only way our discipline will truly be *for* them.

A relationship that close requires that we really know our kids at the heart level. It also requires that we know two other key people as well: our heavenly Father, and ourselves, as we will see in the next chapter.

chapter two

UNDERSTAND YOURSELF AND YOUR KIDS

*For from his fullness we have all received,
grace upon grace.*
—John 1:16

Grace-based discipline relies on understanding that God is our Father and we are His children, and that relationship is the best possible model for how we should parent our kids.

But what if you feel as if you just woke from a coma into parenting? (I do most days.)

Some days, based on their behavior, you look at your kids and haven't the foggiest idea who they really are. And some days, doesn't it seem like you don't even know yourself?

Who are these kids?

All parents look at their little love bundle on the way home from the hospital or adoption agency and are convinced they are bringing home an angelic baby. It doesn't take long before they wonder if they actually brought home Rosemary's baby! Here's the hard truth: your child is a beautiful, shiny, fragile snowflake who is also a sinner.

Think about it. You never had to teach her to throw a tantrum. You didn't have to train him to bite the other baby at the playground who was holding the sand toy he wanted.

When my girls first learned to talk, each of them had the same favorite word: *no*. That was followed quickly by their second favorite word: *mine*. Their language acquisition made quick work of stringing their two favorite words together into a favorite sentence: "No, mine!"

On the other hand, I had to teach them words like *please*, *thanks*, and *sorry*. I had to give lessons in kindness, sharing, and cooperation.

Who Do You Think You Are?

God made a promise to Noah that He would never again destroy the earth with water and strike down every living thing because of mankind. This promise was necessary because God knew that "the intention of man's heart is evil from his youth" (Genesis 8:21). The word *youth* in this verse means infancy. God's promise couldn't hinge on an altered human condition. God's promise to spare the earth His wrath was made in spite of our human condition.

Remember, that's the paradox of a parent, whether that's our heavenly Parent or human parents like us: loving our little hell-raisers right where they are—*but loving them too much to let them stay there.*

We pray, *God, pursue our kids' hearts!* We plead with Him to chase them till He catches them so He can redeem and transform them. Until then, we strive to balance rules and relationship, truth and grace, because guess what? *We are just like our kids.* We share the same sinful nature, even if we've been saved through our faith in Christ. Being saved doesn't necessarily make us any less bratty or sinful. It just makes us forgiven.

Three Inner Needs

Grace-based parenting understands that we all have the same needs our whole lives. Every human heart has three vital inner needs. We all need *secure love, significant purpose*, and *strong hope*.

Secure Love

We need *secure love*. Our need for love only gets met if we experience it from people we trust in ways that make us feel safe. We need to know that the people who love us aren't going to stop loving us based on our behavior or performance.

Significant Purpose

We need *significant purpose*. Our need for purpose only gets fulfilled if we have people in our lives who insist that we are here for a reason, and not a trivial one. We need to know that the reason we were created is to do something that matters.

Strong Hope

We need *strong hope*. Without hope, the inevitable suffering, discouragement, and trials of life will crush us. Without hope, we shun love and forget our purpose. That's why we need more than just a faint vapor of hope. When hope counts, we can't rely on rumor. A strong hope requires people in our lives who believe for themselves and proclaim over us that the hope Jesus offers can't be shaken.

An Ongoing Hunger

These three inner needs—secure love, significant purpose, and strong hope—are absolute. They are not going away any more than our need for food. And like food, it's not enough for us to just *say* to our kids, "I know you're hungry. I'll feed you." We have to actually *do* it.

It's not enough to just *say* we love our kids. It's not enough to just believe on an intellectual level that God created our kids for a purpose and that they can look to Him for their hope. We have to actually feed these things to our kids in a form they can consume and internalize.

Intentions matter, but in this case Yoda is right: "Do. Or do not. There is no try."

Maybe you can relate: my entire life right now consists of cooking food, feeding food, cleaning up food, making sure we have enough food, deciding what food to get, shopping for that food, bringing the food home, and planning what I'm going to make with the food.

Kids eat.

Every. Day.

Multiple times. I have reason to believe that mine think my name is Mom-I'm-Hungry because that's almost always the first thing they say when they see me. They will text me to announce that they are hungry whether I'm on the other side of the country speaking or the other side of the house sleeping.

Physical hunger is not a disease that can be cured with one meal. *(And all God's people said, Duh!)* It's an ongoing biological need. Just like our need for food, our inner-heart needs are *ongoing*. Yet doing our best to meet our kids' ongoing hunger for secure love, significant purpose, and strong hope goes a long way in preventing the type of behavior that necessitates discipline.

We human parents can never meet these needs perfectly. We can't fill these voids completely, and we won't come through every time. These are God-sized needs, after all. Even still, we are the mechanism God uses to meet our kids' heart needs in a tangible way. Parents are the primary reflection our kids see of God's heart and His grace.

The Four Freedoms

We can trust that if God appointed us, then He will also equip us with the right ingredients to assist Him in the work of satisfying our kids' heart hungers.

A healthy diet requires balance, and a healthy relationship requires freedom. Just as we learn to balance out our kids' diets with four food groups, we can learn to give our kids four freedoms: the freedom to be different, candid, vulnerable, and make mistakes.

The Freedom to Be Different

Wouldn't life be so much easier if everyone did things the *right way*, saw the world from the *right perspective*, and valued the *right things*? And by "right," I mean "our." If everyone just did and saw stuff *our way*, then we'd all be winning at life.

Life as clones might be more convenient, but it would also be boring and shallow. It's easy to assume that our ways, our perspectives, and our values are the right ones. Everyone believes that, but we can't all be right!

We rarely have to look farther than our own children to know it's true. It doesn't matter how many children you have; you won't have any two completely alike.

My kids are weird and very often annoying. They hardly ever do things my way, and they rarely approach life from my perspective—facts that never cease to irk me. My husband is no help when I complain about the kids being weird and not doing and seeing stuff my way because he's too busy trying to figure out why the rest of us can't just do and see stuff *his* way!

As long as any of us are stuck being frustrated by our differences, we can't see them for what they really are—gifts! Maybe if God had intended all people to have the same job and fulfill the same purpose He would have created clones. But since He needs us to do many jobs and fulfill many significant purposes, He created us as different as those roles and paths demand.

As long as we see *our way* as right and anything that varies as *wrong* rather than just different, we'll miss the artistry and unique design that God envisioned for those around us. We also might make the mistake of trying to legislate our preferences. We might codify *our way* into the family rulebook, and doing that often has disastrous results.

And, Lord help us, we've all probably had times when we legislated *our way* and then had the gall to call it *God's way*. This is legalism. If we make a lifestyle of it, legalism not only makes the short term uncomfortable for our kids but it can drive them away from God in the long run.

Once we change how we view differences, rather than be constantly annoyed, we'll be able to treasure the strange-to-us, unfamiliar stuff about our kids that defines who they are. This is hard to do, though, because it's deeper than just recognizing that some humans are morning people and some are night people. It's more than just accepting that some of us are dog people and some are cat people. More often, it seems as though the people sharing our home are aliens.

That's likely because they're from a *different country*.

Let me explain what I mean.

At Family Matters, we like to say that people come from one of four primary "countries"—according to their unique personality types. You may have heard the four personality types referred to by other names, but to make it easy for parents to remember, we call them Fun Country, Perfect Country, Control Country, and Peace Country. These are four distinct, sovereign "nations" that make the differences we perceive in one another more than just preferred ways of living our lives, but *completely different jurisdictions*.

- **Fun Country** people value fun, adventure, and excitement.
- **Perfect Country** people value precision, attention to detail, and order.
- **Control Country** people value influence, leadership, and independence.
- **Peace Country** people value cooperation, diplomacy, and conflict resolution.

In the project you'll do following this section of the book, you'll learn about a tool from Family Matters called the Kids Flag Page.[3] This assessment will help you identify the different "countries" that you and your kids hail from. Once you identify each family member's home country, you'll learn how letting each family member live under the sovereignty of their own flag will lend a richness to your shared experience and will declare a ceasefire over your home.

Our kids need the freedom to be different yet still be fully, securely loved.

The Freedom to Be Candid

As we give our children the freedom to be who God created them to be, we must also allow our kids the freedom to be candid—the freedom to tell us what's on their minds, even if it's something we might not want to hear. But there is an important distinction between *candor* and *honesty*, at least the way we often use the word. Too frequently, someone says something cutting and justifies it with, "Well, I was just being honest."

That's not what I'm talking about here. Unbridled honesty usually implies that all our filters are removed and we end up saying hurtful words we can't ever get back.

3 Mark Gungor and Tim Kimmel, *The Kids Flag Page™* (Neenah, WI: Life Discoveries, Inc., Laugh Your Way America, LLC, 2010–2011).

Candor, on the other hand, is honesty that is wrapped in loving-kindness. It means saying hard things in gentle ways.

Ask yourself if you think your kids feel free to be candid with you. This applies more to kids with some level of verbal skills, but do your kids feel they have the freedom to engage you in a respectful dialogue, even if they plod clumsily through it, about things you've done that hurt, frustrate, or embarrass them? Do they feel free to respectfully share opinions that differ from yours?

When our kids frustrate, annoy, or hurt us, it's safe to say that we don't feel any inhibition to let them know. Hopefully the way we do that is with candor rather than unbridled honesty, but I confess I mess this up at times. Without coffee onboard I'm virtually guaranteed to mess it up.

The freedom to be candid usually goes only one way, from parent to child, and not in the other direction unless we cultivate it in our kids. Our kids need to be able to trust us with everything, and that includes the hard things they need to say to us. They've got to believe that saying hard things won't erode our love for them.

The evidence they usually look to is how *we* respond when our child's other parent is candid with us, a point that's sobering and convicting to me because I don't love hearing from Mike that I've acted or spoken in a way that hurt or angered him. I'm not great at admitting when I'm wrong because, truly, I rarely am. I'm much better at getting defensive and proving I'm right!

If the concept of candor is completely foreign to you, if you didn't even realize it's possible to say hard things without spewing bitter words on everyone within earshot, then your kids have probably never seen a healthy model of candor. But, without the freedom to be candid, our kids will stuff things, repress feelings, and bitterness will take root. Giving our kids a respectful outlet for these feelings will keep their hearts tender and able to receive love and discipline from us.

This skill does not come naturally to our kids because it doesn't come naturally to us. It requires both courage and restraint—two things most adults struggle to muster. We can expect that practicing candor will be even harder for our kids, but practice is the only way any of us get better. And our kids will only feel this freedom if we grant it to them.

Our homes need to be places where our kids are free to practice candor without it costing them.

The Freedom to Be Vulnerable

We have a sweet little dog named Mabel. When we walk in the door Mabel flies around the corner as though she were fired from a cannon. She's only about a foot tall, but I honestly think she believes she might be able to jump high enough to lick our nostrils if she tries.

After her hyperactive greeting, she will sit, look up at us, and flop on her back with her legs in the air and belly exposed. We've reinforced this behavior because she's so adorable that we can't help but stoop down and give her a belly rub.

Dog behaviorists will tell you, though, that this isn't primarily an invitation for a tummy scratch (though it's appreciated), but it is primal dog-speak for: *I trust you, Alpha.*

In canine language, your dog is telling you that they recognize you're more powerful than they are and in a position to do them harm, but they're willingly exposing their most vulnerable parts as a sign of deference and dependence.

They're trusting that although you're powerful, you're also good.

What's weird about Mabel is that after we scratch her little dog belly, we can walk away and sometimes she'll stay like that for a long time. I'm pretty sure she's a biscuit short of a full box because we can walk back to our rooms and change, come out to the living room, sort the mail, and look up in the entryway and there she is: still flat on her back, legs in the air. I have to go release her from that hold. I say, "Okay, Mabel!" And she springs back to life.

I didn't teach her that. Heck, I can't teach her not to pee in the house, so I definitely didn't teach her to stay on her back until I release her.

I don't know why I'm telling you this except that my dog is weird (read: different) and also to say that we need to give our kids the *freedom to be vulnerable*. They need to feel safe exposing their soft underbelly of fears, concerns, doubts, weaknesses, and liabilities to us, their "alpha." Like Mabel, they might hold that position of vulnerability for a long time. They might stay in that vulnerable posture for longer than we understand. But they'll only do it if they believe we won't use our position of power to wound them.

By the way, from our kids, this vulnerability doesn't always *look* as adorable as little Mabel frozen upside down in the entryway.

- Sometimes it looks a lot like lashing out in a tantrum or a rage-cry.
- Sometimes it's a series of questions wrapped in self-doubt or unbelief in God.
- Sometimes it's a confession that they're struggling with dark thoughts or poor choices.

Vulnerability is our kids showing us the things about themselves that they hate the most, that they wish they could change but can't, to test if we'll be repulsed or accepting.

My younger daughter, Lydia, has ADHD. I was pretty sure about it from about the time she was three because watching her was like playing back a tape of my childhood. Even at three, other children—neurotypical children—could sit for some period of time at the library's story hour. I know because I've watched them. And my older daughter, though she was an energetic toddler, is neurotypical. Sure, all preschoolers get antsy at some point during story hour, yet the other kids had a baseline capacity to sit, look, and listen.

Everyone except Lydia. She wasn't still for a nanosecond. She'd be standing, walking around, doing a headstand, and peeling a poster off the wall before the librarian opened her mouth. I'd quietly remind her to sit and she'd nod her head and say, "Okay, Mommy." But before her bottom reached the mat she'd already forgotten what she was supposed to do.

Every teacher from kindergarten on gave us the same feedback at her parent-teacher conferences: *Lydia is so smart. She's kind, loving, trustworthy, creative, imaginative, articulate, and absolutely, completely unable to produce any work on her own.*

Sure, they're all just young kids, and they all lose focus and forget what they are supposed to be doing, but what a neurotypical student could do in a fifteen-minute period with three prompts from the teacher required thirty prompts for Lydia. (That's not an exaggeration. I have it in writing.)

Lydia's teacher would remind her, and before she'd even put her little hand on her scissors to cut out the shapes on her worksheet, she'd already forgotten what she was supposed to do.

School, for Lydia, is a microscope on her greatest weaknesses and struggles. In a school setting, her disabilities in executive functioning (the mental self-regulation produced in the prefrontal cortex of the brain) appear in stark relief. Most kids with ADHD, especially girls, lose the physical hyperactivity symptoms as they grow, and Lydia did. She eventually developed the capacity to sit still. But her hyperactivity just went underground. Her brain was just as chaotic as ever. I know because mine still is.

By the fourth grade, Lydia was only a shell of her happy, witty, energetic former self. She'd had wonderful teachers who worked hard with her and who did their best to help her learn. Bless them for loving my daughter well. But Lydia knew she wasn't keeping up. She knew she couldn't get her work done and hold on to her thoughts like the other students. She worked hard every day and was getting nowhere.

The reality that she was going to have to spend the next decade walking into the place where her greatest weaknesses were on display and where no amount of effort seemed to help her do better had broken her down. She was now battling not only ADHD but depression too.

After a particularly hard day, I went in to put her to bed and she said, "Mom, I can't do this anymore. I really think I want to go and be with God so that I don't have to struggle anymore."

Hearing your child even hint at those thoughts, even suggest for one second that she wants to die, is every parent's greatest fear.

A war cry was about to erupt from my chest, but the Holy Spirit washed over me and I calmly said, "Oh, honey. It's that dark? It hurts *that much*?"

"Yes," she said.

I told her that the longing she felt for heaven was okay. That Jesus and heaven are the hope perched on our shoulder as we battle in this life. I vowed that we wouldn't let her suffer at school any longer. I promised that we'd get her help and that her dad and I would do whatever it took to make sure her brilliant brain didn't disappear behind her ADHD, but she'd have to keep fighting alongside us.

She promised that she would, we prayed, and I kissed her good night. After I shut her door, I walked down the hall like a corpse and told my husband what she'd said and we both wept until we had nothing left.

Lydia exposed the underbelly of her darkest thoughts that night. She showed me her scariest desire to see what I would do. Maybe some of you have had this experience too. And only by God's grace can we respond in a way that lets our kids know they are free to share their vulnerabilities with us and we will use our power not to wound them but to protect them.

That isn't what I did at first. I didn't use my power carefully or lovingly when my daughter started showing me her vulnerabilities. Waiting until Lydia was in the fourth grade to get her help is one of my biggest regrets. After listening to every teacher, every year, tell us Lydia was struggling, we blocked it out. I let my pride stop me from getting her diagnosed and treated, because accepting the diagnosis and treatment meant admitting that I had it too. (We are clones in this way.)

When I was a kid, we didn't know as much about ADHD as we do now, and doctors weren't as skilled at treating it. My parents did the best they could with what they knew and how they were advised at the time. But I knew Lydia was struggling early on because I recognized it at a deep level.

I actually had the thought that if we got her treatment (which for ADHD often means medication) and if that medication actually worked, then that meant I had suffered needlessly in school. I wasn't prepared to do the emotional hard work of grieving my own years of struggle, so I turned my face away from my child's suffering. Jesus, forgive me.

The wake-up call we got by way of Lydia's dark admission was a turning point for her, for me, and for our family. It started us on a process of diagnosis and treatment for our ADHD. (Yep, I needed to put on my oxygen mask before I could put on hers.) And make no mistake: it was a process. All the tests, therapies, interventions, and medication trials were sometimes painful, and there were lots of days it felt worse before it felt better.

During the third quarter of sixth grade, Lydia brought home her first certificate for the honor roll. Today she's back to her joyful, funny, confident self, and her potential outshines her ADHD.

Also, you're reading this today because I sought treatment for myself. This book is just one manifestation of the potential that was imprisoned in my brain by my ADHD. Writing a book is something I never would have been able to do before I got treatment. The pill Lydia and I swallow every morning unleashes our brilliance, the stuff that has always been there but has never been able to get loose.

Halleluiah that *our* Alpha never uses His power to wound us when we show Him our underbelly. Our weaknesses are still there. God hasn't taken them away. (ADHD can be *managed* but never *cured*.) It's for exactly that reason Lydia and I can now boast in our ever-present weaknesses because they give God's power a place to land.

Because Lydia felt free to be vulnerable with me that night, both she and I were set free from the prison in our chaotic minds.

The Freedom to Make Mistakes

We all need freedom to make mistakes, even the big ones. Our homes have to be places where even huge mistakes don't cost our children our love. Mistakes might cost them other things because choices have a price, but even when we have to discipline our kids for bad, even sinful behavior, they need to be assured of our love.

Forgiveness goes a long way. Forgiveness doesn't mean that our mistakes have no consequences. It means that we give one another the things we desperately need but don't necessarily *deserve* after we've made a mistake—love, value, and hope.

I've asked God to forgive me for putting my own fears, comfort, and pride ahead of my daughter's by refusing to get her help as soon as I knew she needed it. He's poured out His forgiveness on me. I've also sought Lydia's forgiveness for letting her suffer because I didn't want to grieve my own struggle, and I've apologized to Riley and Mike as well because there was a significant amount of time, structure, and attention that was stolen from them as a result of letting ADHD devour Lydia and me. They suffered too. Mike and both girls have forgiven me quickly and completely.

The longest holdout was *me*. To forgive myself, especially when I hurt the ones I love the most, is the hardest. I have to forgive myself again anytime I think about it. Maybe you're in the same place—struggling to forgive your own mistakes—and if so, all I can say is you've got to let those things fall into the rushing flow of God's grace.

Grace, when we give it to ourselves first, helps us shirk off the bonds of our enemy—perfectionism—and courageously respond when our kids' behavior sounds the alarm.

As we strive to fill the three inner needs that every child is born with (love, purpose, and hope) and offer the four freedoms to our children that God offers to us (freedom to be different, candid, vulnerable, and make mistakes), we create an atmosphere of grace in our home. That gracious atmosphere keeps their hearts primed for grace-based discipline.

KIDS FLAG PAGE

Are you ready for a project?

I know. That sounds like the last thing you need.

Just remember that raising these kids is the most important, and hardest, thing we'll ever do. They are our magnum opus.

That's why we all need to ask the Lord to inject hope into our anxiety and gumption into our stride. We'll need to take the information presented in the previous chapters about relationships, excavate the truth God has revealed to our hearts through it, and put it into real-life practice.

Getting to know your kids better will help you meet their heart needs because you'll be able to better translate your intentions into a language they understand. Knowing what makes your child unique will help you celebrate their differences. One way you can do this is by discovering your kids' unique personality strengths and preferences—what we call their "home country" and "adopted country." I highly recommend doing a full Kids Flag Page assessment on all of your children so that you can identify all of the different countries and jurisdictions that different members of your family are operating under.

You can purchase the Kids Flag Page materials here: fmlymtt.rs/kidsflagpage

The Adult Flag Page is an online assessment that goes more in-depth in certain areas and uses descriptions geared more toward adults. Consider doing an assessment on yourself and, if you're married, on your spouse.

You can purchase Adult Flag Page online assessment codes here: fmlymtt.rs/flagpage

If you plan to use the Flag Page assessments on your kids as well as yourself and your spouse, there is a Family Flag Page bundle that can save you money: fmlymtt.rs/flagpagebundle

What Are the Four Countries?

The four countries are descriptions of dominant personality traits, motivations, and values. There are no "bad countries." All countries are good, God-designed, and God-ordained traits that He programmed and intended for us and our kids. The Flag Page assessments help you to anticipate both the strengths and pitfalls of each unique member of your family.

The following lists describe the traits of each country.[4]

- Fun Country—Never a dull moment, optimistic, inspirational, good on stage, great sense of humor, loves people, curious, sincere, thrives on encouragement.
- Perfect Country—Persistent, perfectionist, unique, artistic, musical, organized, sensitive, faithful, deep thinker.
- Peace Country—Competent, steady, sympathetic, easygoing, patient, peaceful, avoids conflict, good listener, watches people.
- Control Country—Strong willed, bold, born leader, tons of confidence, self-sufficient, goal setter, quick to action, independent, unemotional.

Most of us have a dominant country, which we call our "home country," and a subdominant country, our "adopted country."

---

4   Tim Kimmel, *Discover Your Child's Heart with the Kids Flag Page* (Scottsdale, AZ: Family Matters, 2009), 77, 83.

People are a unique blend of their home and adopted countries and no one fits every description perfectly, but as the graphic below illustrates, when home and adopted countries combine, there are six main combinations that represent profiles of the people that make up the world's greatest workers, the world's most lovable people, the world's strongest-willed people, the world's best entertainers, the world's best owners/managers, and the world's greatest leaders.

Based on what you have read so far, and the Flag Page assessments if you purchased the kit, answer the following questions:

- Which country do you believe is your child's home country?
- Which country do you believe is your child's adopted country?
- Which country do you believe is your own home/adopted country?
- Which country do you believe is your spouse's home/adopted country?

- What expectations are you placing on your kids that might cause your child to feel they are being forced to live outside their home country?

- In what ways is your child struggling with areas you think can be traced back to their God-ordained country?

- In what areas have you elevated your country's preferences at the expense of other members of your family? In what ways are you forcing your country's strengths and motivations on other members of your family?

- In what specific ways are you actively seeking to meet your kids' three inner needs—secure love, significant purpose, and strong hope?

- Pray and ask the Lord to bring to mind if there is an inner need that is not being sufficiently met in any of your kids, a way that they are struggling. Does God bring anything to mind? If so, brainstorm ways you can begin to meet those inner needs.

- Which of the four freedoms—freedom to be different, candid, vulnerable, and make mistakes—do you most struggle to grant in your home?

- Do you think your kids feel deficient in any of the four freedoms? If so, which one(s)? What can you do to fill up those deficiencies?

- Considering your home/adopted country and your child's home/adopted country, what are some ways that you have been trying to meet/express inner needs and grant/accept the four freedoms that are getting lost in translation between family members from different countries?

Write down an action step that you commit to take to affirm your child's unique blend of home and adopted countries.

_____

_____

_____

_____

_____

_____

_____

Write down one way you will commit to change your approach to parenting and relating to your kids based on what you have learned about their home and adopted countries so far.

_____

_____

_____

_____

_____

_____

_____

_____

PART TWO

ESTABLISH CLEAR RULES

Relationship without rules leads to resentment.
—Tim Kimmel

chapter three

CREATE YOUR FAMILY CODE

You shall love the Lord your God with all your heart and with all your soul and with all your strength and with all your mind, and your neighbor as yourself.
—Luke 10:27

My brother Colt says you can ask any firefighter in his engine company, "What are the Big Three?" And with hardly a breath, that firefighter will recite:

Rule #1: Survive.

Rule #2: Prevent harm.

Rule #3: Be nice.[5]

These values are imbedded in the men and women of the Phoenix Fire Department from their first day at the academy. Their commanders want them to be able to list the rules anytime, anywhere, as if their lives depend on it . . . *because they do.*

Colt's "fire family" can easily call out the rules. They know the overriding principles that govern every dilemma they're faced with. It made me wonder if my kids could do the same.

---

5 Phoenix Fire Department Mission Statement,
https://www.phoenix.gov/fire/about-us/mission.

An Impromptu Experiment

A few evenings after learning about the firefighters' rules, an idea struck me. I'd conduct an impromptu experiment. I'd ask my daughters to list our Murray Family Rules and record their answers in my journal.

I thought it would be cool if their answers helped me craft a profound list of family rules to share with you. I hoped that the values my husband and I had worked so hard to impart to them over the last umpteen years of their lives would easily spill from their mouths.

Since I wanted to try to be like a real scientist and not let one lab rat's answers skew the other's, I called my daughters into my room one at a time to ask if they could help me with some research.

Here's the screenplay:

My firstborn walks into my bedroom, where I'm looking over the top of my reading glasses like an overeager shrink.

ME. Riley, if you had to list the Murray Family Rules, what would you say they are?

Blank stare.

ME. Let's say, hypothetically, there was a new family member and you needed to give them a list of our family's rules. What would you tell them?

RILEY. Mom, are you pregnant!?

Blank stare from me this time.

RILEY. You said we have a new family member. I'm just trying to wrap my head around this.

ME. No, and look up the word *hypothetical* later. Focus, honey. What are the rules?

Riley rolls her eyes. I see the gears start to crank in her head. My pen is poised over an empty journal page. Almost faster than my shorthand, she rattles off:

RILEY.

- When FaceTiming boys, always leave the bedroom door open.
- Don't cut your hair in the sink.
- Never leave crumbs or scissors on the couch.
- Respect your parents and the ocean.
- Don't feed the dog red-and-green M&Ms.
- Don't color your sister.

She draws a whistle-breath in, and I take that pause to hold up a stop-sign hand.

ME. Wow, Ry. I'm speechless.

RILEY. That's rare.

I take off my reading glasses and rub my eyes.

ME. Go get your sister, Ry. And don't tell her the question! I want her honest response.

My younger daughter, Lydia, saunters in a few minutes later.

LYDIA. Riley says you want to see me? Am I in trouble?

ME. No, I just have a question. Pretend we have an imaginary new family member, and you are giving them the grand tour of our house . . .

LYDIA. Imaginary family member?

ME . . . and it's your job to tell them the Murray Family Rules. What would you tell them?

LYDIA. What did Riley say?

ME. I can't tell you that.

LYDIA. Her list looks long, Mom. I can see through the journal page.

ME. Yeah, but I want to know what *you* would say.

LYDIA. This feels like a test.

Me. It's not a test. It's just . . . research. I want to know your thoughts.

Lydia. Seriously, Mom! I can't think of anything. Riley gave you enough already!

Riley is peeking around my bedroom door enjoying the show. I shoot her a look, tapping my lips with the blunt end of the pen to signal her silence.

Me. Lydia, what's something that I always say to you? Like, if you don't know what to do, it's that "golden rule" you can count on?

Lydia takes in a long breath. I recognize her slow-motion windup. It's usually followed by a profound quip and a mic drop. I'm hopeful she'll deliver.

Lydia. Never pass up an opportunity to go to the bathroom?

I pictured this going differently in my mind.

You know what happens when you assume? Don't even say it. I already know. I want to go back in time and *bless my own heart.*

Clearly, I'd made some incorrect assumptions.

First, I assumed that my girls had somehow read my mental manifesto of Murray Family Rules. I assumed they could hear my inner monologue and articulate what I'd not explicitly communicated to them.

Second, I assumed that kids have *any* natural desire to make their parents look good.

Oh my gosh, you guys. Do kids not realize people write books on discipline? Do they not care that the people writing said books need anecdotes to make it clear the author is winning at parenting?

I'm asking for a friend.

If at First You Don't Succeed

We needed to try again. A different approach was warranted this time, so we held a Murray Family Summit—a meeting of our minds to explore our perceptions about rules. (All right, fine. I bribed everyone with soda and fancy snacks.)

I asked the kids to brainstorm some important family rules, and this is what they said:

- "Always check the expiration date on the milk."
- "Don't dive into water when you can't see the bottom."
- "Paisley is not a color."

Mike asked the girls, "What about 'Always tell the truth' or 'Never give up'?"

One said, "Those aren't *rules*. That's just how we live."

Or at least how we should, I thought.

While it's encouraging that our girls don't think of moral values as rules so much as a lifestyle, their answers to the question I posed during my first failed experiment illuminated the fact that there are different types of rules. Even the word *rules* has a wide range of definitions depending on who you ask.

Riley seemed to think anything she'd done recently that either annoyed her dad and me or resulted in an undesired outcome needed a rule attached. "Don't cut your hair in the sink" and "never leave crumbs or scissors on the couch" were certainly helpful in a specific time but weren't exactly universal truths.

Lydia, on the other hand, seemed oblivious to the fact that there *were* rules. She only knows that, especially on road trips, she ought to take every chance to make a pit stop. (I don't disagree.)

During our mind-mapping of rules at the Murray Family Summit, I saw some patterns emerge. Once I adjusted for silliness (the AFS factor) by eliminating rules I labeled "immature attempt at humor" and "come on, now," three basic categories of rules emerged.

House Rules

"Chores must be done on Saturday before you can attend social activities" and (my personal favorite) "Finish the open box of cereal before you rip open a new one" fall into the category I call house rules. House rules are legitimate and necessary to help a household (or classroom, business, or city) run smoothly because they set guidelines and communicate clear expectations. But as much as we all think our way of doing things *should* be the law (seriously, *nine boxes* of unfinished cereal in the pantry), we've got to see house rules for what they really are: subjective and negotiable.

Some House Rules are Based in Practicality

These house rules help us maintain balance or accomplish an important goal. They also help us prioritize our responsibilities. Examples of practical house rules include "Children are not allowed to watch television or play video games until they complete their homework each night" and "No phones at the dinner table."

Some house rules are based in preference.

These house rules help us create the kind of environment in our lives that we feel most comfortable in. They allow us to go through life as we prefer. "Load the plates in the dishwasher with the tops facing left" and "Bills go in the 'Need to Pay' folder in the file cabinet" are preference-based house rules.

Preferential Pitfalls

The pitfall inherent in preference-based house rules, though, is that none of us exists in a vacuum. The house we are trying to set rules for is inhabited by *other people*, as if any of them will let us forget! And since we are families, not clones, I'll wager there's a 98 percent chance that every person in the house has different preferences.

I'm a nutcase about how the pantry is organized, but if I put bills in a file and then stick that file in a drawer, I might as well light them on fire. In my mind bills in a closed drawer no longer exist, and I've already forgotten to pay them. I'm a visual organizer, so out of sight is out of mind!

Mike has Excel documents he considers works of art. I look at a spreadsheet and part of my soul dies.

Riley keeps her room neat as a pin. Lydia keeps her room more like a pigpen. During the many years they shared a room, we had to negotiate a balance so each daughter could feel as comfortable as possible in her space. Lydia had to do more frequent cleaning than was her preference so that Riley didn't lose her mind. Riley had to tolerate more clutter than she would in her own space so that Lydia could display her toys in a way that brought her joy.

The girls have their own rooms now. They are allowed to choose how they decorate and organize them. Riley's room looks like a Pinterest board and I rarely have to ask her to clean it. Lydia's room looks like a combination horse stable/alchemist laboratory/ Jackson Pollock painting. But unless we want to start attracting roof rats, the house rule is that Lydia has to muck out her stall on a weekly basis. Making her do it daily would be like my husband making me enter the grocery list into a food-budget spreadsheet. It would kill our dreams.

Needless to say, by about Tuesday afternoon each week I walk by Lydia's room and get a clenching feeling in my stomach. It takes everything in me to choose to just shut the door until Saturday.

Some House Rules are Based in Strategy

These house rules help protect us from our own weaknesses or develop better habits. An alcoholic might have a strict policy not to keep liquor in the house. I know if I even see Oreos I've already eaten the whole box, so I don't buy them and I don't allow them in my home.

Strategic house rules can be tools to help us abide by moral and biblical standards and avoid situations that require more wisdom and restraint than we currently possess. For example, teens are not permitted to go to parties where there's no responsible adult supervision.

These strategic house rules are prudent when they're used to set us and our kids up to be victorious over our temptations and weaknesses. They tend to have powerful motives behind them, so they almost seem like absolutes, but they're not. At least they shouldn't be.

Flawed Strategies

In the garden of Eden, when the serpent Satan asked Eve if God *really* said they weren't supposed to eat of the Tree of the Knowledge of Good and Evil, Eve said, "We may eat of the fruit of the trees in the garden, but God said, 'You shall not eat of the fruit of the tree that is in the midst of the garden, *neither shall you touch it*, lest you die'" (Genesis 3:2–3, emphasis mine). Eve added a strategic house rule to God's words (*don't even touch the tree*) and tried to pass it off as His command. Because of her pride, Eve put her words into God's mouth. She treated her strategy as equal to God's law. She relied on her plan and her power rather than asking God to help her follow His plan by trusting His power. Eve is the Bible's first example of the pitfalls of legalism. And if you read the narrative of Genesis 2–3, Adam just stood there like a lug while Satan had his way with Eve. Adam is the Bible's first example of the pitfalls of license.

Now, no harm, no foul if Eve had said, "God said we aren't supposed to eat the fruit of that tree. I love God and want to obey Him, but I know my weakness to temptation, so to help me obey God, I've decided I'm not even going to touch the tree."

Let's say Eve decided not to touch the tree, but she didn't have a problem with Adam touching it. If it didn't fluster her if he leaned against the tree, it would further prove she recognized the difference between her strategy and God's command. As long as she didn't force her strategy on Adam under the guise of God's endorsement, then no problem.

Also no problem if Adam said, "My wife is feeling tempted by the forbidden fruit. I'm not, but I love Eve and I want to support and protect her. I know that when I'm close to the tree, she notices and she thinks about eating the fruit. That's why I've decided I'm not going to touch the tree either."

But the story of Eden contains none of those alternate realities. The narrative suggests darker motives from both Adam and Eve.

When House Rules Become Toxic

Any house rule can become toxic if we treat it as an absolute. House rules erode our relationships when we think that our practicality is more important than love, our preference is more important than our spouse's, and our strategy is a substitution for God's power.

Our kids' hideous fashion choices or gag-worthy hairstyles might make us itchy because we think they look ridiculous. We'd prefer they *not* look ridiculous. But make no mistake: God cares about hearts, not hair. It's not a spiritual issue.

I've learned from mistakes made along the way that evaluating my kids based on how much embarrassment they cause me or how well they submit to my strategies and preferences only drives a wedge between our hearts. I've decided a better approach is to pull out the camera and document everything so I can put together a gloriously embarrassing wedding montage video someday!

One more thing: sometimes house rules become toxic because we just have too pickin' many. Nobody's perfect, so more rules are just more opportunities for us to screw it up. It shouldn't be lost on us that firefighters have boiled everything down to three rules.

Safety Rules

Some of the rules we listed during our Murray Family Summit fell into the safety category. "Don't open the door unless you trust who's on the other side," "Let only real-life friends follow you on Instagram," and "Never put your face near a dog's face" were a few of our stand-outs.

Safety Rules are Designed to Protect Us From Danger

The world is a risky place, and kids don't usually have very well-developed danger radars. Physical harm can befall them quickly. No matter how invincible your twelve-year-old son thinks he is, skateboarding off the roof presents a fundamental risk because, physics.[6]

Sometimes *people* are risky too. Not every person our kids encounter has their best interest in mind. Evil is a real thing that too often prevails in our fallen world. When it comes to our kids' physical, spiritual, and emotional safety, setting clear rules

---

6 My brothers tried this several times. It never ended well. The fact they tried *more than once* gives you a sense of middle school boys' onboard decision-making skills.

to protect our kids from dangerous people is not only wise but loving. Our kids might not always understand or appreciate them, but ultimately, safety rules help our kids feel . . . well, safe.

Common sense tells us that girls and women are at greatest risk for physical, emotional, and sexual violence. Parents of girls might make more rules that emphasize body safety, self-defense, and emotional boundaries. I know that's true for us and the young women we are raising.

Porn is a headhunter. Our kids don't have to go looking for it; it's looking for them. Pornography is a danger to everyone, but boys and men are at greatest risk that pornography will sink its claws into their minds and hearts. Parents of boys might set more rules about web browsing[7] than they do about walking places alone.

Make Kids Safe by Making Them Strong

Most safety rules are specific to our situations. There are many variables that factor into the big picture of our families and which dangers we're most concerned about. The level of tolerance each of us has to risk is personal. When it comes to inherent risks, the margin for error is sometimes wide and sometimes nil.

That's why grace-based parents realize that the best way to raise safe kids is to raise strong ones. In the same way that building strong immune systems requires exposure to enemy microbes so our systems can properly identify and eliminate the invaders when it really counts, exposure to a certain level of real-life hazards and risk builds our kids' wisdom muscles and bolsters their discernment system.

When our children are born they need us for everything, and they need us to protect them from everything. I'm talking about not only physical protection but also emotional and spiritual

---

7 For four digital laws to help you navigate and guide your kids' choices online, see Appendix A.

protection. Over time, we need to *protect* our kids less so we can *prepare* them more. Those two factors, protection and preparation, have an inverse relationship. In order to increase one, you must decrease the other.

One of the best things we can do as grace-based parents is to ask God to show us specific ways to give our kids a controlled level of exposure to peril and risk so they will become strong and confident enough to withstand inevitable future threats.

When Safety Rules Become Toxic

If we hover excessively over our kids, we end up undermining the very thing that protects our kids the most. If we let our fears drive us, we will end up with weak, defenseless kids. I don't think any of us *wants* to be a helicopter parent. It's exhausting! But we do it in spite of ourselves because, too often, we've swallowed this lie: *the inherent risks we face daily are bigger than God.*

When we believe this lie, we let our fears grow bigger than our faith. When we assess risk and make rules based less on facts and more on our fears, then we are making fear the idol we worship. Power given to fear is merely an unsuccessful attempt to steal it from God.

The good news for all of us is that God is still in charge, He still has the power, and He is always good. We've just got to remember.

---

8   Tim Kimmel, *Why Christian Kids Rebel* (Nashville: Thomas Nelson, 2004), 195.

Moral/Biblical Rules

The third category we saw emerge from the Murray Family Summit was moral/biblical rules. These rules exist so that we know how to live according to God's will. God reveals to us His will through His Word, which sets moral standards for us to observe and boundaries for us to thrive within.

Moral/biblical is the most vital category of rules, yet following them is often harder than any other type for two reasons:

1. We struggle to obey God's clear directives when they involve huge steps of faith, self-sacrifice, delayed gratification, or courage because we stink at that stuff.
2. We struggle to respect God's boundaries and live according to His standards because it's not always clear to us what they are.

The Ten Commandments are clear directives from God. They are moral laws, given to Moses by God thousands of years ago, that still apply today. We struggle to follow them, not because they are ambiguous or veiled in mystery, but, again, because we stink.

Yet not all of God's standards float to the surface as easily as the Ten Commandments. If God's Word is our ultimate family code—our instruction manual for life and our training manual for parenting—but we aren't clear on what it means, then it's going to be really tough for us to get the most out of it. It's going to be even tougher to set clear family rules based on God's Word and discipline our kids according to its boundaries and standards.

We've got to develop wisdom and push deeper to hear God's voice. In the next chapter, I will teach you to recognize the "Three Ps" when you read the Bible. They'll bring a tremendous amount of clarity as you read God's rulebook. Until then, let's look at how we can go wrong when applying moral/biblical rules to our home.

When Moral/Biblical Standards Become Toxic

God's commands and His truth are never toxic, but a misuse of the law can have a toxic effect on us, our families, and those around us. We must remember how Jesus responded when a lawyer asked Him the *greatest* commandment:[9]

> "Teacher, which is the greatest commandment in the Law?" Jesus replied: "'Love the Lord your God with all your heart and with all your soul and with all your mind.' This is the first and greatest commandment. And the second is like it: 'Love your neighbor as yourself.' All the Law and the Prophets hang on these two commandments." (Matthew 22:36–40 NIV)

Jesus doesn't throw away the law. It's still the law. It's just that He knows our tendency to use the law as a weapon and the truth as a measuring stick to gauge the righteousness of ourselves and others, and that's when things get toxic.

That's why Jesus tells us what we need to do with the law: *hang it on love.* Specifically, we need to hang it on a love for our holy God that expresses itself in a sacrificial love for others.

Grace helps us base the rules of our home on love and have an outward-focused relationship with God and others.

Our Family Code

It took several pots of coffee and a few ibuprofen for Mike and me, but the Murray Family Summit motivated us to codify our family's purpose and communicate well-defined principles that, someday, I hope we can all recite as instinctively as the firefighters name their rules.

We developed a family mission statement:

> *Because we are loved by God, we commit to be people who love God and love people.*

---

9 It is of note that the lawyer was enlisted by the Pharisees to use his skills of argumentation to try to trap Jesus into saying that the law and commandments didn't matter anymore. It didn't work.

Then we defined exactly what several key words mean to us:

Love—a commitment of my will to your needs and best interests regardless of the cost[10]

Success—doing what you set out to do; often composed of thousands of failures

Failure—trying unsuccessfully to do or make something; should be seen as a valid option and enlightening opportunity; an important and expected ingredient in success

Learning—gaining knowledge and wisdom through both success and failure

Defeat—giving up

Grace—giving someone what they desperately need, but don't necessarily deserve

Courage—when you're scared to death but you saddle up anyway[11]

After crafting our family mission statement and agreeing on definitions, we wanted to write our family's rules, but we didn't feel as though we had to notate every house and safety rule. We felt sure that with an overarching standard based on God's Word and tempered by His love and grace, the practical and tactical house and safety rules would be made clear to us, and our kids would probably be more inclined to follow them.

Just as Joshua declared, "As for me and my house, we will serve the Lord" (Joshua 24:15), this is the song my husband and I committed to sing over our home and our children.

---

10 We inherited this definition of *love* from my mom and dad and their book *Grace Based Parenting* (Nashville: Thomas Nelson, 2004).
11 We swiped this definition of *courage* from John Wayne (johnwayne.com) because he said it best.

Murray Family Code

Rule #1: Forgive.
Be quick to seek, grant, and accept forgiveness.
Rule #2: Be Brave.
Face your fears, especially when it's what's
required to do the hard, but right, thing.*
Rule #3: Be Kind.
Treat other people like the treasure they are to God.*
Rule #4: Keep Your Promises.
Be careful not to overcommit,
but once you've made a promise, keep your word.*
Rule #5: Work Hard.
Always put your best effort behind what you do.*
Rule #6: Help Others.
Whether family, friends, teammates, coworkers,
teachers, or neighbors, look for people who need help, then give it. *
Rule #7: Never Give Up.
Never give up on people or relationships.
When a task seems too hard, stick with it and ask for help.*
Rule #8: Trust God.
Believe that God is who He says He is
and He can do what He says He can do.*
Rule #9: Tell the Truth.
Always tell the truth, no matter how hard it is to tell. Staying silent
when you know the truth is the same as lying.*
Rule #10: Live Authentically.
Be the same person in the dark as you are in the light.*

*When you mess up, refer to Rule #1.

chapter four

BASE YOUR RULES ON GOD'S WORD

Your word is a lamp to my feet and a light to my path. I have sworn an oath and confirmed it, to keep your righteous rules.
—Psalm 119:105–106

Ask my kids, "What is Mommy's life verse?"

They'll recite, "Whoever blesses *her mommy* with a loud voice, rising early in the morning, will be counted as cursing" (Proverbs 27:14).[11]

I love that verse so much. I've always dreamed of getting *Loud Voice + Morning = Cursing* embroidered on a pillow that I can chuck at my kids when they violate my favorite ~~moral/biblical~~ house rule.

Making my kids memorize my life verse was going well for me until they started reading the Bible on their own.

You should start in Proverbs because there's one for every day of the month, *I said.* It will be great, *I said.*

On day twenty-seven, Lydia found my life verse in the actual text. Hawkeye that she is, she realized I'd substituted the word *mommy* for what was actually there, which is the word *neighbor.*

---

11 Gender-changed pronouns and my paraphrase in italics.

"It says here that blessing your *neighbor* with a loud voice in the morning will be counted as a curse. *Neighbor*. Not mommy."

Starting to crouch low, I offered, "Yeah, well, it's still always true."

Lydia said, "Well, not *always*. I mean, what if your neighbor's house is on fire? What then?"

Shoot. She's going to be a litigator someday, I just know.

She plowed forward with her cross-examination. "Then using a loud voice could save them, and no one would curse you for that!"

By this point, I was fantasizing about drowning out her words by suffocating myself with the imaginary embroidered pillow.

It wasn't the only time I've tried to twist a Bible verse to serve my purposes, but it was thankfully the most benign. Take my word for it: twisting Scripture should be avoided. Our kids are smarter than we are, and when they find out we're trying to use the Bible to serve our own desires they might end up resenting us, or the Bible, or both.

In all seriousness, if we are going to base our moral absolutes on the Bible, we need to be clear about what the Bible says—and what it doesn't say.

Reading the Bible Is a Required Course

If you say Theology 101 is boring, I appreciate your honesty. If you'd rather skip it, you're not alone.

But, in all love, we've got to get over it. This is a prerequisite all parents need to take. I'm taking *myself* behind the woodshed here too. I'm wagging my own finger in my own face.

As parents, raising our kids is the most important job we'll ever do. Most of us have spent more time reading our life insurance policies than we have the Bible. We take training courses or employ life coaches to help us hone our professions and trades, yet we neglect reading the most important job training manual, the most valuable life coaching book ever written: God's Word.

We don't need seminary degrees, but if all we ever do is a keyword search in our Bible app, that won't cut it.

Playing Bible Roulette won't cut it either. You might not know the term, but you've done it. We all have! Here's how it works: You're desperate for *something* and racking your mind for an *answer*. You've tried everything else, so you breathe a quick prayer like a gambler blows on dice, riffle through your Bible, and put your finger on a verse. You're hoping that random verse will be the miraculous answer you need.

God is good because, *even in this*, the Holy Spirit often speaks to us despite our rubbing His Word like a genie's lamp.

Other times, the Bible Roulette wheel lands on something like, "Your two breasts are like two fawns, twins of a gazelle, that graze among the lilies" (Song of Solomon 4:5).

Bible Roulette just got weird. Especially if you're a dude.

Cherry-picking the Bible is *usually* better than no Bible,[12] but it's far better to learn to really read it so God can speak to us through it.

I struggle to muster the self-discipline to read the Bible regularly. Many of you are at a stage of life where you are rarely able to use the restroom without an audience. I get it. I'm only just on the other side of those years myself. It's hard to get time to spend by ourselves for *anything*, let alone reading the Bible on a regular basis. I know I *should* promote a Bible-in-a-year reading plan or some other structured format, but since I constantly fall on my face with those formats by about mid-February each year, I have no business assigning that task to you.

If a structured format appeals to you, awesome. But if you constantly fail at those, like me, that's okay too. Stop beating yourself

---

12 But not *always*. See Exodus 21:15.

up, because guilt and shame shouldn't be our primary motivators for reading God's Word. God should be our motivator. Spending time hearing Him speak to us should be the draw.

At your stage in life, you might only be able to ingest a small morsel of Scripture a day, but just keep at it. Get an audio Bible you can listen to in the car or while you do other things. Or put a Bible in your bathroom in the rare event you get a few minutes to yourself so you can read a bit. Jesus will always meet you, *even there.*

That said, the Bible is vital and necessary in learning our trade of parenting. You need a crash course that will help you wherever you're at. Even though I constantly need a refresher in this course material myself, indulge me for a minute and let me play teacher.

Also, let me borrow a pen!

The Three Ps

A grace-based home sets the expectation of living by God's standards so we can fully experience the joy that living within God's will brings. We want to avoid the pitfall of making things moral or spiritual issues when they're not. So as we begin the process of setting clear boundaries and expectations, we want to be sure to put the house rules, safety rules, and moral/biblical rules in the correct categories.

The best safeguard is what I call the "Three Ps." As we read the Bible, even if it's just a small morsel, we should ask: "Is this a *precept?*" "What *principles* should I apply to myself and my family?" "Do either of my answers need to change in light of the current biblical *precedent?*"

Precepts

Biblical precepts are *God's commands that He means for all people at all times.* They are universal laws and you're under their jurisdiction no matter who you are, where you're from, or when in history you're born.

Identifying commands in Scripture is pretty straightforward because commands are usually stated using clear, declarative language. Phrases like, "You shall/shall not," "I command you," and "Do not" tend to precede a commandment of God. Yet identifying a *precept* is not as straightforward because not all of God's commands are precepts.

Some commands in Scripture are given to specific people at specific times and weren't intended to be followed by all people in all times. That's why we have to examine even some "shalls" and "shall nots" through accurate historical, cultural, and literary context in everything we read. We've got to view each piece of Scripture through the lens of the whole Bible.

For example, in Matthew 19:16, a wealthy young leader asks Jesus, "What good deed must I do to have eternal life?" Jesus says, "Keep the commandments" (v. 17).

The guy asks Jesus to clarify which ones, and Jesus starts calling out the Ten Commandments, *all of which are precepts*: "You shall not murder, You shall not commit adultery, You shall not steal, You shall not bear false witness" (v. 18).

The man stops Him. The guy's basically all, "Yeah, yeah, yeah . . . I've followed all those and more in my youth. What more must I do?"

Then Jesus answers him with another command: "If you want to be perfect, go and sell all your possessions and give the money to the poor, and you will have treasure in heaven. Then come, follow me" (Matthew 19:21 NLT).

The man is grieved because he is rich, so that command stinks for him. He walks away.

The Lord wasn't speaking in metaphor (although He frequently used metaphors when He taught). He wasn't suggesting the rich man should sell everything he owned figuratively (although he often used figurative language). The rich man asked Jesus a direct question and the Lord gave him a direct, literal answer.

Does that mean if you and I want to get into heaven we have to sell everything we own and give the money to the poor?

When we look toward the greater context of the Bible, we see plenty of people who gained eternal life who didn't follow that command literally. Abraham amassed a whole nation of descendants, land, and wealth, yet the gospel writer Luke refers to Abraham as being with the angels (Luke 16:22). The Old and New Testaments detail countless God-honoring people—people we have every reason to believe we'll see someday in heaven—who didn't follow the "sell everything" command. Both rich and poor people enter the kingdom of heaven.

So, is the "sell everything" command a precept?

A command is only a precept if it's intended both literally and *laterally*, meaning to all people across all time. Jesus's "sell everything" command was given specifically to the rich young ruler, not to all people.

Principles

Biblical principles are *underlying truths we can glean from any part of God's Word to help us live according to God's will.*

In reading the passage about Jesus answering the rich young ruler, we need to ask the next question: "What *principles* should I apply to myself and my family?"

All through the Bible there is evidence that God wants us to take care of the poor and be generous with what we have. Greed is condemned and generosity is blessed. Even though the "sell everything" command wasn't given to us specifically, there are principles—underlying truths—we can apply to our lives.

God's truth is layered and plural. So while this is not the *only way* the passage can be applied, when I read the exchange between Jesus and the rich young ruler, one principle that grabs me is: Jesus wants to be Lord of the man's life. He wants to be more important to him than anything else.

Jesus knew the rich young ruler treasured his wealth—and the power and influence that wealth afforded him—above all else. That's why Jesus's command grieved the man so much. Jesus was asking him to drop what he tight-fisted so he could give his whole heart.

Jesus asks the same of us, only the treasure we tight-fist might be our career, our beauty, our freedom, or even our family. Even good things need to take a seat so Christ can have the stage.

Precedents

Biblical precedents are *documented examples and events that set a new standard, pattern, or benchmark for the future.*

Keep in mind: all precedents are examples, but not all examples are precedents.

The last essential question we need to ask of anything we read is: do either of my answers ("Is this a *precept?*" "What are the *principles?*") need to change in light of the current biblical *precedent?*"

Thinking of the Bible as one book is a common mistake. It's sixty-six individual books written over more than fifteen hundred years by more than forty Holy Spirit–inspired writers. The context, culture, and covenant recorded over the course of these sixty-six books *progresses*, and biblical precedent progresses along with it. Nowhere is this more evident than the way precedent progresses between the Old and New Testaments.

The word *testament* means covenant or contract. The Old Testament—the old contract—between God and His people (Israel) was rewritten. Because of His love and according to His will, God wrote a *new* contract, with *new* terms: the New Testament (covenant).

Good News: New Terms

Every precept and principle in Scripture must be viewed in light of the most relevant biblical precedent, which for believers is the New Testament.

In the new covenant, *God's people* are redefined to include not just the Jews but everyone who calls Jesus, Lord. In order to execute this new contract, God allowed mankind to execute His Son. Jesus signed His name on the dotted line in blood. He gave His own life as the final sacrifice required for the forgiveness of sins.

Let me be clear that I'm definitely *not* saying Old Testament precepts and principles are void in light of the New Testament. It's just that all the Old Testament rules are now subject to the new biblical precedent, one that has progressed toward its ultimate expression: the new covenant. The law has a new qualifier, or a new precedent: grace.

> For sin shall no longer be your master, because you are not
> under the law, but under grace. (Romans 6:14 NIV)

Grace is radical. Breaking the rules is still wrong. It will still get you into trouble and bring you sorrow. The wages of sin is still death. But the new covenant includes a clause that says even when we earn death, God pays us back with forgiveness and eternal life if we accept His gift of salvation by making Jesus our Lord (Romans 6:23).

That's why my family's Rule #1 is "Be quick to seek, grant, and accept forgiveness." And there's an asterisk next to all our rules to remind us that when we mess up, we refer to Rule #1.

The Cost of Confusing a Precept and a Principle

Growing up, we knew a family that lived as though the "sell everything" command was a precept. They centered their entire family philosophy on that *one* exchange between Jesus and the rich young ruler. Their kids could recite it verbatim and the parents referenced it constantly.

Their family creed, which they'd often cite, was, "God owns everything. He gives us our daily manna. Everything beyond that we give to the poor in service to the Lord."

I'm in no position to judge these parents' intentions or question their devotion to Jesus. I can only tell you how I saw their family creed play out in real life.

They never owned a home or car. They rented houses and apartments, borrowed cars, and went through seasons of staying with friends and family.

The dad never held a steady job. He said a job tied him down too much and he felt called to be a hometown missionary rather than to pursue traditional work.

Their kids were never allowed to accept gifts. If birthday or Christmas gifts *did* make their way home with the kids, those items were quickly given away to "the poor."

The kids didn't have clothes, toys, or beds that were truly theirs. Everything in their home was considered community property.

When they did have to buy clothes (and that's only if the Lord didn't provide those items through a friend or relative whom they asked), *they had a mandate to buy only from garage sales or thrift shops.* New items purchased from a retail store were considered a "waste."

The parents never had money to pay for medical care. They asked doctors in their church to treat their kids for free.

Their fridge and pantry rarely had any food in them. They lived, quite literally, hand to mouth. The kids would frequently come over to our house hungry.

When their mom *did* have to go grocery shopping (if the Lord didn't "provide" the food some other way), *she wouldn't buy anything that wasn't on sale or that she didn't have a coupon for.*

The kids never had any money to go on field trips or buy school supplies.

They always had to request scholarships to church camp. In fact, they thought it was wrong that the church even charged a registration fee for camp—that's what *tithing's for*, after all.

When it was time for the kids to go to college, *there was no savings and the kids had to fend for themselves* either by taking out loans or simply not going.

Those kids must have thought our house was Disneyland when they came to visit. They'd run straight to our rooms and marvel at our toys, try on our clothes, and lay in our beds. They'd chow down food as fast as my mom could fix it.

Over dinner, their parents would keep bringing the conversation back around to how they were serving the poor and how much they were able to give back because of their chosen lifestyle. One night, I'm pretty sure it was my little sister, who was around five or six years old at the time, who said, "Um . . . isn't *you guys* 'the poor'?"

She put words to what I'd always wondered but never said. She put her innocent little finger on the fact that the family who talked so much about serving and giving to the poor, *are the poor* who were asking others to supply their needs, by choice.

This family's story is an extreme example, to be sure. Most of us don't go to this extent. Yet, I share it because it illustrates the folly of confusing precept and principle, as well as failing to consider new covenant precedent as we approach Scripture.

When Good Intentions Backfire

I have the benefit of hindsight now as I reflect on this family's history. I know the outcome of their lifestyle choices, and it hasn't been good. The kids from this family are adults now and, overwhelmingly, they resent the way they were brought up. They'll tell you they never felt any sense of security. They never knew where their family would be living, where their food would come from, or if they'd get help when they were sick. Their communal living stripped them of any sense of privacy and autonomy, and their scruffy clothes, lack of school supplies, and constant requests for school or church to pick up their tab made them the objects of constant ridicule. They might have been able to overlook all that, except they knew it was all their parents' *choice.*

Their parents drilled into them that God was their Provider (which is true). Yet they saw the other kids at church. They saw families who loved the same Jesus and worshipped the same Great Provider. But those families never seemed to struggle as their family did. The other families had stability and abundance. So, as kids are prone to do, my friends assumed Jesus must not love them as much as other families since He didn't provide for them as abundantly.

My friends longed for the stability they saw in other families. But that longing was consistently met with righteous indignation from their parents, who said they needed to have more faith, because living a radically sacrificial life serving the poor was more important than their comfort. It might have been a sincere conviction on their parents' part, but it forced the kids to wrestle with things they weren't ready for. They looked to their parents for comfort, security, and stability—and *never got it.* Their resentment of their parents ultimately shaped their view of God.

As adults, all but one of these kids turned their backs on the Lord. The one son who still professes faith in Jesus has fought an uphill battle with doubt and belief. As a reaction to his parents, he's made some unwise decisions along the way that have left him scarred. He's reluctant to have children of his own now because, despite his disdain for their parenting style, it's all he knows and he's afraid he'll become just like them.

The Truth Versus the Whole Truth

Before I offer any more analysis of what I think went wrong in how these parents interpreted the Bible and established their parenting philosophy, let me give these disclaimers and clarifications:

- There's nothing wrong with renting (rather than purchasing) homes or apartments. *I've done both.*
- Unemployment and underemployment are real and debilitating. *We've all lived through the Great Recession.*
- School trips, activities, supplies, church camps, medical care, and keeping food in the house are crazy expensive. *There've been multiple times when we've had to ask for scholarships or our parents' help.*
- There's nothing wrong with borrowing stuff instead of buying it yourself. *I borrow my friends' boats and mountain cabins as often as they'll let me.*
- The amount of presents kids get for birthdays and Christmas is out of control. *I often feel nauseous at the excess. We could all use more restraint in this area.*
- Financial planning is tough but important. *If you looked at our savings account right now, you'd either laugh or cry.*
- Student loans are a reality for even the most financially conscientious parents because tuition costs are astronomical.

My husband and I will be fortunate if we get his school loans paid off before we take out new ones for our girls!

- Being frugal is part of good financial stewardship. *I shop with coupons, almost half my wardrobe is from a resale store, and nearly every piece of furniture in my house is from a garage sale or a thrift shop.*
- Caring for the poor and serving sacrificially are biblical mandates. *My heart breaks for folks who have far less than me, and the gospel requires I help anytime I can.*

I acknowledge all of these legitimate points. These are real struggles and to each I offer, "Me too." But make no mistake, I had choices. I had options available to me that many families don't. Too many hardworking, loving parents are poor and have no choice. Poverty is something they are trying to escape, not a spiritual movement they can opt in or out of.

If pleasing God requires us to choose poverty, then tell that to every kid who has gone to bed hungry without a choice. Tell that to the single mom whose heat was turned off in January and had no option but to cradle her child under every blanket, towel, and piece of clothing in the house to keep from freezing.

It's the truth that we can serve God by choosing a simple life and giving to the poor, but it's not the whole truth.

My friends' parents established their family creed based on a myopic view of the truth. I believe the way they lived it out was shortsighted, and ultimately, the experiment failed their kids. On the surface, their goals seemed noble. Voluntary poverty *is* a spiritual gift, but it's not the only one. Theirs certainly *can* be a noble lifestyle, but it's not the only way.

Their good intentions backfired because, rather than viewing the isolated conversation Jesus had with the rich young ruler through the lens of the whole Bible and subjecting it to new covenant precedent, that single passage became their lens for everything.

To them, voluntary poverty became a badge and serving the poor became their god. Jesus says we are to care for the poor, but He says a whole lot of other stuff too.

It's vital to establish a family code based on grace. We must make the Great Commandment—love God and love people (Luke 10:27)—the axis that everything in our homes hinges on.

Learning and applying the Three Ps as we read the Bible protects us from using God's Word as a weapon and His law as a measuring stick for the righteousness of those around us. It helps us discern how to establish in our homes the rules, boundaries, and expectations that point toward God's holiness and also reflect His gracious heart. It provides wisdom and perspective when our kids break the rules or skirt the boundaries and we must discipline them.

And it prevents us from cross-stitching our disdain for morning people onto throw pillows.

DIY RULE BOOK

In the previous chapters, I told you about the Murray Family Summit and the haphazard way that experiment began. I shared that my failed experiment was the catalyst for what ended up being an enlightening, edifying, and transformational time for our family.

We also had a crash course in reading the Bible to help us better discern how to apply it to our family's rules and creed. We saw how basing those family philosophies on anything other than grace can backfire.

In the end, we produced a document that helps shape our family culture and will guide us through tough decisions we're sure to face in the future. Our family mission statement, defined terms, and the rules we live by make up our Murray Family Rule Book.

In this section, I will guide you in the process of developing your own family code and writing your family's rule book.

Your Family Summit

Let's agree to learn from my mistakes and skip the impromptu rule-quiz I gave my girls that fateful night and, instead, follow this intentional plan to host your own Family Summit.

Pro tip: There's nothing wrong with bribery in the form of tasty food.

Schedule your Family Summit at a time when you can be as relaxed as possible (I'd say "well rested," but ... LOL), and where all members of your family will feel free and safe to contribute their ideas. You might have to break up the brainstorming portion into smaller segments of time with young kids. I suggest kids three and under be exempt and can just smear brownies on their faces and run amok.

If your kids are old enough to participate, their input can be illuminating, as it was for me. Also, if your kids are anything like mine, this will be the time to manage your expectations of their input a little better than I did. Don't forget to bring your sense of humor.

Three Simple but Not-So-Easy Steps

1. *Mind-Mapping*: Start by writing down every rule that comes to mind during brainstorming.
2. *Sorting*: Place each brainstormed rule into one of three columns: house rules, safety rules, and moral/biblical rules.
3. *Analysis*: After you've categorized all your rules, spend some time (either as a family, married couple, or alone) analyzing the columns of rules.

Analyzing Rules

There are three main questions about your rules that you need to honestly and prayerfully explore: "Are the columns balanced?" "Is every rule truly in the correct column?" "How do I view the moral/biblical rules?"

I have to warn you that the analysis step can be painful. You'll need to be brave. When my husband and I looked at our rules, we saw areas where we were out of balance and several places where we'd put rules in the wrong columns. It was painful to ask the

Lord to show us *why* we'd made these mistakes. When we took honest looks at our own hearts, the Holy Spirit put His finger on a few sore places.

Healing sometimes hurts and growth often involves growing pains, but blame and shame are not invited to your Family Summit! They will consume your joy and hog the guacamole. Give yourself, your kids, and your spouse lots of grace. I know that you can do this because I know that God will equip you if you ask.

"Are the Columns Balanced?"

- Are your lists heavy on house rules but light on moral/ biblical rules? Is that because you are placing too much weight on practicality, preference, and strategy and forgetting the biblical precepts and principles that should govern those rules?

- Is your list so long on safety rules that your kids never get a chance to build their strength physically, emotionally, or spiritually? Are you letting your fear grow bigger than your faith? Are you swallowing the lie that the risks our kids face are bigger than God?

- Do you have too few rules (or none) in any or all columns? Is this because you think that rules (in any category) are trivial and unimportant?

- Do you simply have too many rules in any column? This sets everyone up to break them. Try to prioritize the most important in each category. Focusing on character and key principles in each category will usually negate the need for the other rules. (Refer to the list of character traits starting on page 108.)

"Is Every Rule Truly in the Correct Column?"

- Pay close attention to the moral/biblical column. This is where it's easy to mislabel house rules that are very important to us.

- Are you treating your preference-based house rules as non-negotiable (especially if you're a perfectionist) when they are completely arbitrary? As much as we think "cleanliness is next to godliness" *should be* in the Bible, it's not. Perfection is not a biblical imperative. On the contrary, God goes out of His way to make sure we understand that perfection is impossible for anyone but Him. Recognizing our own brokenness is absolutely necessary for repentance and salvation.

- Even *more* tricky: Have you mistakenly put strategic house rules in the moral/biblical category? This usually happens when these strategic house rules help us to obey a moral/biblical rule. This is what Eve did when she said they weren't supposed to touch the tree. That was a strategy-based house rule, and it would've been fine if she'd kept it in the right category, but she put it on the same level as God's command and tried to put God's stamp of approval on it.

"How Do I View the Moral/Biblical Rules?"

- Do you view the moral/biblical rules like a to-do list? Moral/biblical rules are action-based (meaning, they are things you do/don't do), but we have to be careful not to fall into the trap of seeing them as things we must do out of obligation, but rather as ways that we can respond to God's love.

- Do you view the moral/biblical rules as a self-improvement plan? Viewing moral/biblical rules as self-help is bankrupt because as much as we try, we will fail. These rules aren't ways to do better or be better. That's not the point of the moral/biblical rules. God put them in place to ensure our joy, because He knows that consistently living outside of them steals our joy.

- Do you use the moral/biblical rules as a weapon? Are they stones you gather to beat others (spouse, kids, friends, yourself) over the head with blame and shame? The Bible says, "Judge not, that you be not judged" (Matthew 7:1). The rules aren't there to brutalize us or our loved ones. The rules exist to increase our joy.

- Do you use the moral/biblical rules as a measuring stick? Moral/biblical rules are not a way to determine if other people are measuring up. That's not our job; it's God's. The Bible says when we accept the forgiveness and atonement that Christ's death on the cross provides, God then measures us by Christ's righteousness! God doesn't measure us by these standards—and if anyone has a right to judge us, it's *Him*! These rules are simply ways we can respond to the love that God has for us. God loves us and desires us to experience joy. He sets standards He knows will protect us from choices that rob our joy. Our obedience is simply a love offering back to God.

- Do you trivialize the moral/biblical rules? Do you resent them as something that weighs you down? Is it because you think God is some cosmic killjoy trying to kill your fun? Is it because you feel guilty since you've blown it, so you think you might as well quit caring? I promise you, when you really get to know your Father, when you let Him love you, you'll see that none of that is in His character. He did not send His Son to condemn the world but to save it (John 3:17)!

PART THREE

RESPOND WITH GRACE

We are a lighthouse, permanently established to show our kids the way home.
—Tim Kimmel

chapter five

EVALUATE EACH VIOLATION

For all have sinned and fall short of the glory of God.
—Romans 3:23

I was grocery shopping a few weeks ago. I looked at my cart full of groceries and thought, *Yep. That's everything I need.* Then I just pushed my cart out to the truck. As I loaded everything in the back, I wondered why in the world they hadn't put it in bags.

Then I realized it's because I forgot to check out!

If I'd been caught at that exact moment, I could have been legitimately prosecuted for shoplifting a week's worth of groceries. But, in this case, context and intentions matter.

Fortunately, the store was gracious when I walked my contraband back inside and explained that mommy fatigue had caused my brain to go all *Walking Dead.*

Sometimes our kids do stuff that looks, in the moment, like a crime. But grace says we'll take time to understand the context of their actions and uncover their intentions before we decide if they're jailbait.

It's All in Our Heads

At the beginning of this book, I shared a mental exercise I use to help me separate my child's behavior from her heart so I can see her a little more as God does. When I imagine gathering up all the annoyances, bad behavior, rule violations, and sin and putting them in a basket, and then walking it into another room and putting it up on a shelf, it helps me diffuse my own strong emotions so my brain can go back to a place where I'm thinking rationally. This exercise helps me *respond*, rather than *react*.

The second part of the mental exercise, after getting our emotions in check, is deciding how to respond to the behavior we just put in our basket. In this chapter, we will start going through our baskets and analyze what's inside and what's not. By learning to categorize what's in our baskets, we'll be better able to prioritize (since we can't and shouldn't respond to everything), and we'll be able to more effectively and more quickly respond.

I use the basket exercise in the moment of a child's misbehavior, and I also use it after the fact to help me process the events of a particularly hard day. When you're in a moment of behavioral crisis with your child, the time frame in which you run through this visualization might be mere seconds, but often that's all it takes to calm our emotions.

The second part of the exercise—deciding what, if anything, you need to do about the behavior—takes more time and practice. This is where using this exercise retrospectively, like while lying in bed at night, allows more time to process what's in your basket and to formulate appropriate responses. It serves as a mental rehearsal that catalogs those well-reasoned responses in your parenting muscle memory so you're able to access them more quickly and correct or redirect more appropriately next time you face a similar crisis with your kids.

It's like practicing your parenting ninja skills by cover of dark so you'll be able to combat your kids' unacceptable behavior with speed, accuracy, and stealth the next day.

A Basket of Bother

There is really only one criteria for what goes in the basket: *it bothers us.*

Whatever our kids were doing made us too emotional to think. Their behavior frustrated, angered, annoyed, hurt, saddened, or scared us, so we put it in our mental basket and separated it from their heart to help us see our kids through God's loving eyes.

In order for this mental mechanism to work as intended—to deescalate our emotions—there can't be any other qualifiers. If it's bothering you to the point of overwhelming emotions, you're not thinking and you can't respond, so the behavior goes in the basket.

Yet, once we regain a calm mind, because of such loose standards for what we toss inside, we need to take time to analyze the contents of our basket. Often the stuff our kids do that bothers us most is minor in the big picture of life. And because we're focused on those minor but majorly irritating behaviors, we're less bothered by the choices and behaviors that are a huge deal from an eternal perspective.

We need to take inventory of what's in our basket.

Your daughter's loud music before your morning coffee is a squeaky wheel. Your son's forgetting his lunch on the counter for the third time this week produced a surprisingly strong emotional reaction. Unfortunately, the behaviors that bother us and therefore end up in the basket don't always warrant a response. They might, but they might not. There's not always a correlation between the two. That's because emotions aren't accountable to logic or reason, and that's okay. It's not an indictment of our emotions; it's just how they work. Emotions only feel; they don't think. That's not their job.

We also must take inventory of what's not in our basket.

Since there's not always a predictable correlation between what bothers us and what's important, we can't assume that the behavior and choices our kids make that do warrant a response—the stuff that matters most in the long term—will even end up in our basket. The basket exists to help us separate behaviors that bother us from our kids' hearts so we don't let our emotions lead and we don't define our kids by their most frustrating, annoying, hurtful, frightening, disappointing behaviors. But often it's the subtle choices, behavior, and sin (the kind of stuff that flies under the radar) that have the most detrimental effect on our kids in the long run. Yet those things don't always end up in our basket because they might not incite our emotions in the moment.

We also might not know about them. The fact that your son copied last night's social studies homework off his seatmate on the bus won't end up in your basket because he omitted that information in the summary of his day. You weren't present to witness your daughter being a bystander while her friend bullied a girl at recess. Don't harbor guilt over this. Goodness knows we moms and dads already have so many unknowns to lose sleep over; we don't need more. I guess that's my point: we only have so much capacity to deal with issues we know about, and we have no worry to waste. Our kids throw such a large volume of stuff at us daily that we don't have the resources to respond to all of it.

That's why we've got to learn to prioritize.

Five Hills to Die On

We've all heard the sage advice: pick your battles. Once we draw our battle lines we ask ourselves, "Is this a hill I want to die on?" When we decide to fight a battle with our kids, we have to see it through. If we surrender too many fights, our kids will start to doubt our resolve and lose respect for our authority. If you have strong-willed kids, as I do, surrendering battles will feed their belief that they ought to be in charge instead of you.

I'm going to build on that age-old wisdom about choosing battles and seeing them through—except that because we're talking about parenting battles, you need to know you're more Super Mario than human. Like a video game character, you have multiple lives that you can expend before it's game over. I don't know . . . five, maybe. Like Super Mario or Pac-Man—you have five hills on which you can fight to the death with your kids. Use them wisely.

Five is just a number I chose because it's one we understand in the context of video game characters. I don't know if it's five or twenty or three; I just know it's more than one. You have more than one hill to die on for your kids, but it's a finite number and you can't do it every day. If you try to, it'll be game over before your kid makes it to kindergarten. Save your strength, because there *will* be battles worthy of your life. There *will* be issues you will face over the twenty-plus years you'll spend parenting your kids that are so serious, you'll need to be willing to risk it all to see those battles through to the end. That's why, in deciding what hills are worthy of dying on, it's important to learn to sort the stuff your kids do in order of seriousness so you don't waste your blood on the wrong hills.

Not All Violations Are Created Equal

Violations, just like rules, have different categories. Recognizing these categories helps us discern what response to give. It will help us see places we're overreacting. It will help us recognize times we're underresponding. We'll have a clearer picture of the battles that warrant our inner warrior and the skirmishes we can safely ignore. And we'll be able to better recognize times when mercy is the best response.

Taking time to process what's in our mental basket might also expose places where we need to ask our kids' forgiveness. Perhaps we've been focusing on all the wrong things. We love our kids and that's usually why we're hard on them. But as we look deeper, we might realize that was the wrong response. More difficult to admit, but perhaps we've been ignoring a quiet cancer that's growing in our kids' lives because we're either too distracted to notice or because the disciplinary surgery required to excise it from their lives seems too painful and messy and we don't want to face it.

If you find yourself in this place, remember how powerful forgiveness is. There's a reason our family's Rule #1 is "Be quick to seek, grant, and accept forgiveness." Forgiveness is the no-fail anti-dote to all our shortcomings, but we need to seek it, give it freely, and often accept it ourselves.

Regulatory Offenses

A lot of the junk you pull out of your mental basket will fall under the category of regulatory offenses. These are actions that aren't necessarily morally wrong, but they violate a statute or rule. In common law, regulatory offenses are things like exceeding the speed limit and not having the proper license to hunt, fish, or drive a car. Going fifty-one miles per hour in a forty-five miles per hour zone isn't morally wrong, but it does violate the rules.

In our homes, regulatory offenses are times when the behavior isn't necessarily wrong in and of itself, but it violates a rule we've set. Just like our society, we need to recognize that regulatory offenses are in a different category than crime.

I told you about our backyard hens, the ones that came with our perfect house with the broken air conditioner. We love them! They're beautiful, their antics are funny, and they turn bugs, weeds, and kitchen scraps into eggs. They're like our own personal backyard soap opera. We have given our hens elaborate backstories, personalities, and life goals. We spend far too much time imagining and discussing the drama in our poultry's social order.

To us, our backyard chickens are somewhere between pets and livestock, and anyone who has owned either knows one thing for sure: chickens are messy, sometimes stinky, and their living area is full of germs.

Taking care of the chickens is a responsibility we all share. (Except for Mike. He's decided to be Switzerland as far as the chickens are concerned.) The girls and I take turns feeding, filling water dishes, collecting eggs, and cleaning out the coop.

On the back porch, just outside the kitchen door, are three pairs of rubber clogs that fit all three sets of feet that go out to do chicken chores. When we're done, we're supposed to leave clogs outside before coming in the house. That's section 7, line 3 of the Murray Poultry Code.

Sometimes, though, we forget to change out of our regular shoes and into our clogs (myself included), or we're outside doing other things and decide to go visit the hens. Even if we aren't doing anything chicken-related, we often step in a "hazard" when we least expect it. If this happens, the code says we take off whatever shoes made contact with the mess before coming into the house. The soles of our shoes need to be rinsed, air-dried, and sprayed with disinfectant before we can wear them in the house again.

All of these code regulations have one important goal: *keep chicken poop out of the house.*

More specifically, no E. coli making its way into carpet fibers, grout, or kitchen counters where it can make us sick.

This is a set of regulations designed to protect us and to maintain some semblance of sanitation in our home. It's also completely arbitrary. Our strategy for keeping chicken manure out of the house (and the fact that we even have chickens at all) is specific to us, and violating these regulations isn't morally wrong; it's just gross.

Of course, my kids have messed this up. I've messed it up. We all get sidetracked and forget what we're supposed to do. It's not a moral issue, but there are still consequences: we have to bleach the kitchen floor, disinfect countertops, and steam-clean our carpets more often. When the girls forget, I often make them do "emergency hazmat cleaning" before they're allowed to do anything else.

A while back, we slipped into a bad habit where none of us were taking the sanitation code seriously. So one day out of desperation I asked my mother-in-law, a biomedical engineer, to come over and show us our chickens' manure under her high-powered microscope.

Gag! We nearly choked on our own disgust.

The close-up image of creepy crawlies that come inside the house on our coop shoes is burned on the inside of our eyelids and has probably been the most powerful motivator for us all to comply with the statute about coop shoes.

Yet we still sometimes forget.

Our Murray Poultry Code has a compelling purpose behind it, but I confess that many other times I regulate and legislate my own preferences, such as cereal-packaging etiquette, maximum volume level of voice in the morning, and proper disposal of dirty socks.

If, as you're processing the contents of your imaginary mental basket, you're mostly encountering regulatory offenses: First, you have a *good* kid. Second, you might have some soul-searching to do.

We Are the Regulators

If we set regulations that are too complex, are too unrealistic, or run counter to the primary way our kids do life (their "home country"), then we are setting them up to be repeat offenders. And we are setting ourselves up to be nagging, nitpicky compliance officers. I don't know about you, but that's not the primary role I want to play in my kids' lives.

We don't want to be the loathsome HOA that dictates every house in the neighborhood be painted Builder Beige and have grass no longer than two and three-fourths inches. Our kids will end up resenting us if we Barney Fife them over every detail of their lives.

Overly restrictive regulations turn otherwise well-intended, conscientious kids into noncompliant violators. In order to comply, they become lifeless robots, or worse, they feel they'll never measure up so they completely give up trying.

On the other hand, removing excessive regulations or changing how and what we regulate can set us all free.

Remember, we (the parents) are the ones setting the regulations, and these regulations are arbitrary. We often have good reasons for our statutes or regulations (such as in the case of house or safety rules) because they help us create order, stay healthy, accomplish goals, or be safe, but they're still negotiable. Breaking these rules isn't disobedience as much as noncompliance.

Misdemeanors

Vandalism, reckless driving, and trespassing are examples of misdemeanors in most judicial systems. Our society recognizes that some crimes, while they are wrong, are less serious than others. Usually misdemeanors cause minimal harm to others, if any at all, and they incur only petty amounts of financial damage. The consequences for misdemeanors are proportional to their lesser damage and are usually fines or community service.

In our homes, misdemeanors might be tantrums, refusing to eat dinner, or getting out of bed after being told to stay (resisting arrest?). Misdemeanors fall on a spectrum of seriousness and often have more to do with our kids' personalities (stubborn refusal of food), preferences (night owl with sleepy parents), or stages of development (toddler or teen tantrums) than anything else.

Unlike regulatory offenses, misdemeanors are more than non-compliance; they're disobedience. The action might be wrong in and of itself, but it might also be wrong because it's direct disobedience of a request or command. True disobedience is something we tend to think of as a serious crime, especially if it elicits a serious emotional response in us like hurt or anger. But it matters *in what way* they're disobeying. Disobeying direct orders might be a misdemeanor depending on what the order was and the context it's couched in.

Minor Misdemeanors

One afternoon, I told my kids not to eat any of the freshly baked cookies on the counter because they were for a Christmas party I was attending that night. What I didn't tell them was that "for the party" meant I was supposed to bring *exactly* three dozen for the cookie exchange. The recipe I'd used had, annoyingly, yielded precisely that many and I didn't have ingredients to make another batch. I didn't have even one extra cookie to spare.

When I got out of the shower and went back to the kitchen to transfer the cooled cookies into a tin, there were only about two dozen left.

I freaked out. I went on a tirade about how I was going to be late now because I'd have to make more cookies. Everyone else seemed to be able to be on time for parties. I was going to be the only schmuck who showed up late without enough cookies. How is it when I say "Don't eat the cookies," they assume I'm saying, "Just kidding! Go ahead and eat a bunch! Please make my life harder than it already is!"?

I reacted. I let my emotions lead. My emotions were fueled by my own insecurities.

Most of my frustration was because I would be late, not have enough cookies, and appear incompetent. We all know Christmas cookie exchanges are really just a front for showing off your baking skills to other ladies, right? Make no mistake: it's a competition. You might not be the best baker at the party, but you can usually feel good that you're not the worst. Except that now I was going to be the one everyone felt better than. The other ladies would be all, "Well, at least we're not eking our way through life like Karis." Happy birthday, Jesus!

My ego-driven, emotional diatribe, as I'm sure you guessed, was a reaction, and not a good one. Sure, I told them not to eat the cookies. They disobeyed. But my reaction wasn't fair and it wasn't gracious.

They didn't know I had no extra cookies. When I bake, I usually make extra so there's margin for tasting and sharing. Usually, it's not a big deal. They figured "don't eat the cookies" meant "don't eat *all* the cookies," so in a moment of olfactory-driven weakness they gave in to temptation and ate a few each.

"Don't eat the cookies" was a direct order. But they disobeyed it because they were hungry and the freshly baked cookies smelled good. I can sympathize with that. Also, they didn't realize how tight my margins were because I didn't take the time to explain. Up to that point, I'd established a precedent of making extra baked goods, so they had reason to think I did this time, especially because I didn't tell them otherwise. A good defense attorney could make a case for entrapment.

Punctuality to a cookie party and my own status in the competitive sport of holiday baking did not matter one iota in the big picture. But if I had not realized my error ... if I'd just let my angry, sarcastic words weigh heavy on their hearts, it could have cost our relationship in the long run.

Fortunately, the Holy Spirit thumped me on the head and reminded me of Rule #1 (forgive). I let go of my anger over the cookies and asked my girls to forgive me for erupting because of my own insecurity and ego.

I was only about ten minutes late to the party. In addition to the two dozen Russian teacakes I'd baked, I brought a package of Keebler Fudge Stripes cookies that I found in the back of my pantry. No one seemed to care. Perhaps the baking competition had all been in my mind.

Serious Misdemeanors

Some misdemeanors are more serious. "Don't hit people" is a rule pretty much everywhere. Depending on the ages of your kids, it might be something you say frequently. Hitting is more serious because it requires a level of intentionality even if it's a "crime of passion." Hitting does real physical harm. It hurts and victimizes another human being. It's also a behavior that crosses the line between misdemeanor and felony, depending on the situation.

In my house, hitting (or any other physical violence) is a misdemeanor *only if* the harm to the victim is relatively minor *and* if it's mostly motivated by overwhelming frustration. To me, it has to meet both of those qualifications. Otherwise, it's a felony.

It's helpful to remember, too, at certain stages of development (such as toddlers) impulse control isn't very good. Your child's impulse to hit Sally when she takes a toy he's holding is easier to control at ten years old than at three. Your three-year-old will probably grow out of most of their violent behaviors. Also, Sally most likely won't be yanking toys away from other people when she's ten either.

Misdemeanors need consequences, but they've got to be proportionate. For us to respond appropriately, we've got to keep perspective. We've got to dish out a correction or consequence if it's warranted and then let it go. Don't stay mad. Don't worry that your kids are going off the rails. You'll have far more worthy hills to die on.

Felonies

In our law systems, felonies are serious crimes because they cause serious physical or financial damage, they victimize another human being in a significant way, or they are so deviant and egregious that they cannot be tolerated in civilized society. Murder, grand larceny, fraud, and negligence that results in serious harm are just a few examples. Because these crimes are the most serious and severe, it's appropriate that they're given the most severe consequences.

In our home we see lying, cheating, defiance, or any type of abuse (physical or otherwise) as felonies. What makes it tricky is that a particular action, like hitting, might be only a serious misdemeanor in one situation but a felony in another. For example, I will share with you a true story, but I'll keep the characters anonymous to protect the guilty.

One of my daughters was frustrated with her sister, so she punched her in the shoulder. I gave her a stern look and a quick verbal correction: "Do not punch your sister in the shoulder."

She looked me in the eye, set her jaw, and jabbed her sister hard in the ribs.

Stuff just got real.

The behavior started as a misdemeanor and could have ended with a stern look, verbal reminder of the rules, and an apology. Instead, my daughter decided to call me out on the battlefield that day.

The same action—hitting her sister—that started as a misdemeanor became a felony because the second time it was premeditated and underscored by an attitude of defiance.

At that point, I confronted her disobedience. She yelled, "You said not to punch her in the shoulder! I didn't punch her there!"

Strike three. Assault, premeditated defiance, and blatant disrespect.

I have a "mama snap" I'm pretty sure can be heard for miles. My mom has one, and her mom has one. With our thumb and forefinger, we can make a noise that wallops the air like Leviathan being released from the deep. After my daughter's final outburst, I gave my mama snap. When she heard it she knew she'd picked the wrong mama to mess with. My little felon took one look at my face, dropped her pride, and ran.

Yes, she did receive a consequence because I love her and I won't let that kind of behavior continue on my watch. I'll push back hard against violence, defiance, and disrespect because if I don't and she doesn't learn to control those behaviors, she'll pay a high price later.

Sorry Yet Serious

I have a friend whose son is a highly emotional, highly impulsive kid. His strong emotions are part of his unique design, and his impulse control (or lack of) is a result of his age (eleven) and personality more than anything else. One afternoon, he and his sister were out in the backyard. He was hitting a softball off a tee, and she was annoying or otherwise infuriating him as little sisters are known to do. So instead of swinging his bat at the top of the tee, he redirected and bludgeoned his sister in the back of her foot. This was not a Nerf bat. His blow shattered her heel.

As soon as his bat made contact with her heel, he felt remorse. His sister was rushed to the hospital and needed surgery to repair her heel and tendon. All afternoon, he bawled for his sister and refused to leave her side even when visiting hours ended.

His mom and I had talked about the concept of misdemeanors and felonies, so later that week, she called me because she wanted to process what happened. We talked about how his crime was committed in a fit of frustration and was not premeditated. He was deeply remorseful for hitting his sister, which I reminded her was good news, because it means he's not a psychopath! (You've got to find humor wherever you can.) She wondered out loud, since he was provoked and because he was so sorry, could she treat it like a misdemeanor?

She and I are close enough that I can level with her. I said, "Other than self-defense or an accident, there is no universe in which hitting someone with a bat and putting her in the hospital is anything less than felony assault."

It didn't matter what his sister might have done or said to frustrate him. It didn't matter that he did it because his emotions got the best of him. His remorse and concern for his sister *did* matter but didn't change the profound degree of harm he'd inflicted. What he did was serious and required a serious consequence. The most loving thing my friend could do was to ensure he never does anything remotely like it again. Consequences needed to be swift, calculated, heavy, and memorable.

Is It a Misdemeanor or a Felony?

When our kids' behaviors and actions are inherently wrong, and when their attitudes are more than noncompliant but full-on disobedient, we still may be unsure how serious these "crimes" are. We know these are not just regulatory offenses, but should we treat them as misdemeanors, or are they felonies? When I'm unsure, I have two litmus tests that shed a ton of light.

The Ten-Year Rule

Whatever the behavior, imagine your kid doing the same thing in a similar context ten years from now.[13] How does the behavior look then? What are the consequences of the same behavior then?

When you're in the thick of it with your five-year-old, you might have a hard time seeing into distant dark corners ahead of you. The ten-year rule can illuminate these for you.

Imagining your kid doing the same thing at age fifteen instead of five might be laughable. It's funny to think of your fifteen-year-old son refusing to take a nap or waking you up before 6 a.m. even though you've begged him not to. If you remember anything about being fifteen, then you know sleep is a favorite pastime of teenagers.

The thought of your thirteen-year-old daughter wailing and throwing herself on the floor in the grocery checkout line over your refusal to buy her a pack of gum is ridiculous (although designer jeans are another story).

If the same behavior ten years from now seems laughable, ridiculous, or highly unlikely, then you're dealing with something that's mostly *developmental* and most likely a misdemeanor. They'll grow out of it.

---

13 My good friend Karina Loewen wrote about this concept and how to use it to pick your battles in "Choosing the Mountains to Die On," Family Matters (blog), June 20, 2014, http://fmlymtt.rs/2bYOYb5

The flip side, though, is that the ten-year rule might illuminate behaviors that *will* cause far more damage and have much more serious consequences in the future if they continue during the next ten years of your kids' lives. Imagine my friend's son who, in frustration, smashed his sister in the heel with a bat. Add ten years to *that* behavior. At twenty-one, an assault like that could land him in prison. Behavior that isn't primarily developmental and could continue ten years in the future if not squelched now deserves our greatest attention, especially if the behavior will cost our kid far more in consequences down the road. These might be the hills worthy of a loving parent's life.

Character Issues

If you're still not sure if you're dealing with a minor misdemeanor or a felony, there's another question you can ask that will guide you: "Is this a character issue?"

This question has two angles:

- Does this behavior display a current lack of character that needs to be built?
- Is this behavior out of character compared to how my child usually lives?

If the answer is yes to either question, then the behavior deserves our focus.

Next questions to ask yourself: *If this character issue is projected ten years into the future, what does it look like then? What do I need to do about it now?*

When your kids are ten or even fifteen, dishonesty, laziness, cowardice, cheating, and quitting can look small and insignificant. These might not be the things that bother us most or elicit the biggest emotional response, so when they're young these issues might not be among the things that end up in our mental basket. A lack of character is a heart issue that can be invisible at times, so it's easy to forget to be mindful, especially when we are focused on more outward behaviors. Yet building character into our kids' hearts is one of the most critical jobs we've been tasked with as parents. You want your child to grow into a man or woman of character because that's what God wants for us, and that's the best preparation for the world they'll face as adults. So, rather than letting these character flaws be swept under the rug because they're not as annoying as other behaviors, we need to coach our kids in development of character and let consequences come to bear when they make poor choices.

In the book *Raising Kids Who Turn Out Right*, my dad identifies six character traits that grace-based parents ought to be intentional to build into their children's hearts.[14] These character traits were the backdrop of my family growing up, and during the Murray Family Summit, we put their definitions into our own words:

- *Faith*—a deep conviction or belief that results in the submission of our intellect, will, and actions to God. Regardless of circumstances, trusting that God is good and that we need Him.

- *Integrity*—who you are when no one is looking. Stopping at the red light in the middle of the night, even when there are no other cars on the road and no one is coming from either direction in the intersection. Telling the truth, even when it comes at a high personal cost to you.

---

14 Tim Kimmel, *Raising Kids Who Turn Out Right* (Scottsdale, AZ: Family Matters, 2006), 34.

- *Poise*—a keen sense of the appropriate. An intuitive wisdom that weighs the needs and best interest of the moment against the backdrop of truth and integrity.
- *Self-Discipline*—being willing to do the hard but right things. Putting momentary pleasures and conveniences at a distant second to doing what needs to be done. Never sacrificing the permanent on the altar of the immediate.
- *Endurance*—seeing commitments through till the end, especially when you want to quit. Keeping your word. Completing what you start. Crossing the finish line even if you are so beaten and battered that you must rely on the shoulder of a comrade to help you across.
- *Courage*—being willing to sacrifice your personal safety to defend the defenseless. Confronting that which makes you afraid with the truth that God is who He says He is, and He can do what He says He can do. Recognizing that fear is a legitimate emotion, but not necessarily the best indicator of what we should do. Fear can inform our response but must never dictate our reaction.

These are the character traits grace-based parents seek to instill in our children. So the next time you ask yourself, *Is this a character issue?*—you can review this list to determine if any of these six key character traits need to be developed further in your child.

Choose Your Battles

The hills worthy of our bloodiest battles are felonies our kids commit that display a lack of character. And remember that while it often seems as if they're the foe you're fighting *against*, they're actually the ones you're fighting *for*.

Choosing which battles we'll fight is one thing. Deciding how we'll respond is another. Grace-based discipline requires not only recognizing the types of violations so we can focus on the right things, but also trying to understand their motivations.

Asking ourselves why our kids do what they do can clue us in to which consequences and corrections will be most effective. It can also help us better see the hidden character issues that we must address.

Uncovering motives is vital to discipline because not only do we need to deal with *what* our kids do, but sometimes we also need to deal with *why* they do it.

chapter six

DETERMINE YOUR CHILD'S MOTIVATIONS

The heart is deceitful above all things, and desperately sick; who can understand it?
—Jeremiah 17:9

Firefighters have only four senses.

At least, they have only four senses they can count on inside a blaze.

That's because the inside of a burning structure is almost always pitch-black. It might seem counterintuitive because we associate flames with bright light, but being inside a burning structure is nothing like we picture it and far from how it's depicted in movies. Complete darkness is the norm.

Think about it: electricity has been knocked out, artificial lights have been destroyed, and smoke pulls a black curtain over everything, even in broad daylight. Firefighters won't really *see* the fire until they're five to ten feet away, and even then it's only a faint glow. If they aren't already anticipating the location of the flames and preparing to take defensive measures, by the time they see it they're deadly close. So, in order to survive, they learn to sense where the fire is by the rising temperature and the growing roar long before they're within range of the flames.

The Academy teaches them to fight fires totally blind. They black out the facemasks in their training helmets. They run drills in the dark. They learn to manage their equipment blindfolded. They hone their senses of hearing, touch, smell, and taste, because they know those are all they can rely on.

Firefighters learn to *see fire without eyes*—they determine where it is, what's fueling it, and how best to put it out. If they don't diligently train their other four senses, they could pay with their lives.

As we process the stuff from our kids that ends up in our mental baskets, we'll need to quickly define the types of violations our kids commit. When we aren't sure if something is a regulatory violation, misdemeanor, or a felony, first we should pray and ask the Holy Spirit for a sense of wisdom. When we face the pitch-darkness inside our disciplinary inferno, like the firefighters, we've got to learn to *see fire without eyes*.

Fighting Blind

We might hear a growing roar of flames when we apply the ten-year rule to our kids' behavior. As we press forward into the pitch-black, we might feel the temperature rising and know we're getting closer to a character issue.

Once we know what type of violation we're dealing with— what type of fire we're facing—deciding how we will respond to our kids' behavior (or if we should respond at all) is even more nuanced. If we rush into the darkness, we can make dangerous mistakes.

We want a script. We desperately wish there was a formula. But since there's no perfect prescription for every scenario we face, we've got to use our senses to factor in the variables so we can respond. One huge variable we need to try to understand is our kids' motives.

Why Are They Doing This to Us?

If you're like me, you might take a step back from something your kids did and ask, "Why in the world?"

It's a necessary question that doesn't always have an answer. Sometimes we don't know. They don't know. *Nobody knows.* There's not always a root cause behind our kids' behavior . . . at least not one we can, or should, do anything about.

We can drive ourselves nuts trying to figure out why our kids do certain stuff (and it's often the stuff that bothers us most), yet there's no clear motive, at least not one that's rooted in some great moral failing or lack of character.

But sometimes their misbehavior might be rooted in a deeper motivation that we need to deal with. If we don't, our response will be like dumping water on flames that keep coming back because we haven't eliminated the accelerant that's fueling them. Let's examine a few of the motivations that might be fueling your kids' behavior.

Developmental or Just Whatever!

I like to file some of my kids' behavior under "Just Whatever." There might be an answer as to why they do this stuff, but I don't know what it is—and even if I do, there's nothing I can do about it right now.

Here's one: kids who refuse to eat one minute and are hungry the next.

You know what it's like. You have to fight for every bite that goes in the kid's mouth. You're begging, negotiating, threatening . . . you make the food she requested to her exact specifications, and then you're practically shoving every bite down her throat. Finally, once she's laid out a convincing case that she can't fit even one more bite in her tummy, you're like, "Fine. Just whatever!"

Just when you've put all the food away, you've washed and put up the last dish, and you've finally turned off the light in the kitchen is exactly the moment your kid walks up to you and says, "Mom! I'm hungry."

Why do they do this to us? Are they trying to break us? Do they get some level of sick pleasure out of making us nuts? I don't know. They don't know. *Nobody knows.* Just whatever.

Maybe she's a picky eater. Maybe she has sensory issues. Maybe she's strong willed and you've made meals a battlefield. Maybe your cooking stinks. There are ways you can deal with some of that, but remember, this is not a moral issue. Perhaps it's a health issue, but probably not as much a problem as you think. Unless they have a genuine medical condition that compromises their system, you really can just let your kids eat dinosaur chicken nuggets and dry Cheerios all day, every day. Kids have the magical ability to still grow on a diet of potato chips. I'm not saying it's ideal. I mean, I'm an organic-eggs-from-backyard-chickens, grow-your-own-fruits-and-veggies, crunchy mom, but even I'm telling you, they will not die if all they eat is pizza.

Also, now that I'm a few miles up the road, I can tell you that along with any of the motives listed above, the behavior is probably also mostly developmental. I mean, when you think about it, depending on their age and physical size, they have really tiny stomachs. Their little tummies fill quickly and they empty just as quickly. It's entirely possible for them to be full five bites into dinner and about to die of starvation fifteen minutes later.

I promise they'll grow out of these shenanigans! They'll grow into new stuff, though. Tweens and teens eat all the time. You won't have to beg them to eat; you'll have to beg them to stop eating! I have a friend with five sons. She goes to Costco three times a week, fills two carts, brings everything home, and her boys promptly eat it all.

Say, "Just whatever!" And try not to go broke.

Another "Just Whatever" behavior: your kids won't stop getting out of bed after you've put them down. Sometimes they get up right away and come to the living room where you're trying to watch the episode of *The Bachelor* you've had saved on your DVR for six weeks. The season's already over and you haven't gotten past the third episode!

Even after you finally get them to sleep, they still find a way to make the great migration into your room. The worst is when you've been asleep awhile and they wake you up in the middle of an REM cycle and you're nauseous and disoriented. You're not sure if you're dead or if this is some type of terrorist hostage negotiation!

Why do kids do this to us?

What was confounding to me was that my kids never got any positive feedback when they did this. Except for the rare times they were genuinely sick, had a nightmare, or wet the bed, I always put them back to bed. Waking me from sleep produces a predictable, frightening outcome. It's like poking a grizzly bear. When I was growing up, my parents used to flip a coin over whose turn it was to wake me up. I definitely did not give my kids a reason to want to wake me . . . yet they did. Every night. Just whatever!

There can be a thousand different reasons our kids get out of bed or wake us once we're sleeping. Sure, it could be a battle of the wills. That's possible. Or they could come into our room because of a bad dream, wetting the bed, being sick, teething, poor sleep hygiene, they're thinking about muffins, they have an itchy ear, or their foot hurts. They don't always know. We don't always know. Sometimes, *nobody knows*.

I can tell you this: they will almost never do this when they're thirteen. Once they fall asleep, you'll have a hard time waking them. They'll be practically comatose. As teenagers, it'll seem like all they do is eat and sleep. They will probably not sneak into your bed in the middle of the night just to cuddle . . . and you might miss it. I hated hearing people tell me that when my girls were younger. I insisted, "I will not miss it." I love my sleep just as much now as I did then, but I do, perhaps, miss them coming to me for comfort at night . . . but only a little.

Hang in there, weary parent! This is not your hill to die on.

Maybe sleep (or lack of it) is the biggest obstacle you're facing right now. You might recognize it's magnifying everything else to the point that nobody is rational anymore. Foothills have become the Rockies because no one in your house is sleeping. Trust me, I'm not making light—lack of sleep is a real, serious thing. Sleep deprivation is how the CIA breaks imprisoned enemy operatives.

This is an instance, though, where it's particularly important not to take your kids' behavior personally. Don't waste a ton of emotional capital on this. They aren't targeting you, even if it feels like it.

Motivation: Stupid

Sometimes our kids do stuff primarily because they haven't grown out of their stupid yet. They have underdeveloped prefrontal cortexes. So they throw a full fishbowl from the second-story landing just to see what happens. Children have a high tolerance for risk and pain, and a low level of discernment and deductive reasoning. Trying to understand why is futile. Just save money for the hospital bills and try to keep them out of prison. These are not hills to die on. Besides, your kids will need you conscious so you can call an ambulance for them.

Motivation: Self

Whining, complaining, entitlement, greed—all are manifestations of the same basic problem: selfishness. We all struggle with selfishness, and our kids are no different. Often, some of the most infuriating behaviors that end up in our basket, especially if we have older kids, are words they say or actions they take based on a selfish attitude that's permeating their lives. While these problems can seem the most deeply engrained and difficult to shift, there's an antidote to attitude, a reset switch that can help rewire pervasive selfishness: service. When any of us struggle with a bad attitude, it's almost always because we are focused on ourselves. The fastest way to change that is to look up and look out. The antidote to attitude is serving others sacrificially on a regular basis. A kid who's struggling with a chronic bad attitude needs an outlet to serve. They need opportunities to volunteer their time, labor, talents, and skills to help others. Serving others also builds our kids' sense of security, significance, and strength because they see that God is able to use them to do great things, both big and small.[15]

Not Wrong, Just Different

Along with the developmental challenges, immaturity, and the "Just Whatever" behaviors, some stuff our kids do that bothers us and ends up in our mental basket isn't wrong; it's just different.

Messes, for example. A kid from Fun Country sees a jar of glitter and thinks, *Fun! Shiny! All the pretties I can make with this! What if it's pixie dust and I can use it to make the cat fly?*

You, on the other hand, might be from Perfect or Control Country. Or you just might not be a fan of trying to vacuum glitter out of the cracks between your hardwood floor planks until

---

15 For a roadmap to raising others-oriented kids who serve sacrificially, see Tim Kimmel, *Raising Kids for True Greatness* (Nashville: Thomas Nelson, 2006).

midnight. Either way, try not to find a moral problem in a kid who's just being a kid.

Try to recognize when the reason your kids are acting the way they are is they are simply existing in their space the way God designed them. You're trying to exist in your space the way God designed you. The problem is that you've got to share the same physical space with your weird kids.

Close bedroom and playroom doors. Maybe create a sacred space for yourself (even if it's in a closet, attic, basement, or the garage). When it all gets to be too much, put yourself in time-out in your sacred space. Breathe. Pray. Chocolate helps too. (For you. Not the kids. Just wanted to clarify.)

Or maybe you're a Fun Country parent, but your kid is from Control Country and you can't understand why they freak out when you decide to be spontaneous and take them to the park in the afternoon instead of staying home and watching a movie like you originally planned. You say, "The park! How awesome!"

Your kid thinks, *The park is awesome, but it wasn't the plan! A movie at home was the plan! This calls for a meltdown!*

Our Control/Perfect Country kids need advance notice if plans are going to change. Stay home, watch the movie, and try to communicate and compromise better next time.

Do not lose your chill over this.

Because They Are Sinners

Understanding our kids' motives is important and worthy of our time. Sometimes we don't know, they don't know, *nobody knows* why they do what they do, because they are young, different, haven't grown out of their stupid yet, or just whatever. This tends to prove especially true of the stuff they do that isn't necessarily wrong, but it violates some rule we've set (or law of physics) or it annoys, inconveniences, or bothers us, so it ends up in our basket.

Sometimes, though, our kids do stuff that *is* wrong. They do stuff *they know is wrong*. They're manipulative, deceitful, unkind, or brutal. *On purpose*. Even in these times, there isn't always a clear cause or deeper reason for their behavior other than that they are sinners.

This shouldn't surprise us, yet it always seems to knock the wind out of me for a moment with my own kids. All throughout Scripture, we're reminded that we're sinners. We're born into sin, it's our nature, and we all need the cure only Jesus provides. Also, if our preexisting heart condition is that it's "desperately sick" with sin, as Jeremiah reminds us (Jeremiah 17:9), then it follows we can't always understand why our kids do sinful stuff. I don't always understand the sinful stuff that *I do*. Ultimately, just like us, our kids need Jesus, His forgiveness, and the sin-cure He offers. God has provided this cure to us by allowing His Son to go to the cross and pay the price we owed on our behalf. Because it has been paid once and for all, like an open tab with an unlimited bank account of righteousness behind it, even those of us who are forgiven and saved keep on sinning our whole lives, and God keeps on forgiving.

The most basic answer is this: our kids do sinful stuff because they're sinners.

There's nothing we can do about this. Sin is not something we can protect our kids from. That's because sin isn't some external force trying to breach the fortress of our kids' hearts. Sin only exists because it dwells in us. We can't protect our kids from sin, because we can't protect ourselves from sin . . . because *we are sin*.

Fortunately, 2 Corinthians 5:21 says, "For our sake he made him to be sin who knew no sin, so that in him we might become the righteousness of God." Our kids need to put their faith in Christ and accept His transformational grace and forgiveness in order to have any chance to resist their sinful nature. Until they do, our efforts will merely be outside-in behavior management. Ultimately, they need inside-out heart transformation.

We can't do this for them, and I caution you against any pressure you might be tempted to place on your kids to "ask Jesus into their hearts." It's vital they arrive at this decision themselves. If they do it to please you, or because they feel they must, they may eventually walk away from their faith because it wasn't entirely their choice. By all means share the gospel with them. Pray for and with them. Let them see you living sold-out-in-love with Jesus. Let them see you reading the Word, and read the Word with them. Bring them to church and involve them in a loving community of Christ-followers. Petition the Holy Spirit to pursue their hearts like a Lion. Pray they will surrender their control and place their faith at the foot of the cross.

Until then, your kids really have no means to resist their sin nature (although negative consequences we administer can influence their behavior), and they'll do stuff we can only attribute to the fact that they're sinners.

Yet we might see behavioral patterns (sinful sometimes, but otherwise just undesirable or not in their best interest) or things that are such a departure from the way they typically live that they give us reason to think there's an accelerant fueling the behavior. And the accelerant needs to be dealt with before anything else will sufficiently put out the fire.

Sometimes There Is a "Why" for the Behavior

In spite of all the motives fueling our kids' behavior that we can't, or shouldn't, do anything about, we aren't helpless as parents. I do believe that sometimes there *is* a "why" behind our kids' behavior that we *do* have the ability to address.

I'll even go as far as saying this is really the only behavioral motivator we should try to do anything about.

I'd like to seed an idea in your mind that might help guide you as you try to formulate a grace-based response to the stuff you're sorting out of your basket. *Sometimes our kids do stuff (sinful or otherwise) because they are trying to meet a legitimate need in an illegitimate way.*

I see at least three categories[16] of legitimate needs our kids might be seeking to meet in illegitimate ways with their behavior: physical needs, special needs, and inner needs.

Unmet Physical Needs

Physical needs include hunger, thirst, tiredness, feeling cold/hot, illness, or pain. When we have an unmet physical need, it starts shouting at our bodies and our subconscious so loudly that it drowns out everything else.

Hangry is a word for a reason. You know its definition if you've ever taken a hungry, overtired child to the grocery store. Whatever restraint or impulse control they had when well fed and well rested is reduced and their threshold for frustration, noise, stimulation, and patience is low.

In the midst of a grocery store meltdown you can, and should, correct, redirect, and discipline their bad behavior, but ultimately, the behavior is fueled by their unmet but legitimate physical needs. They'll use any means to compel you to take them home, feed them, and put them to bed. I don't think our kids, especially the young ones, realize they're doing this. It's a subconscious survival instinct. But it doesn't negate the theory that most of their undesirable behavior in that scenario stems from attempting to meet their legitimate needs in illegitimate ways.

---

16   There could be more than three. I am open to more categories. These are the three categories I see based on my experience.

Unmet Special Needs

Special needs your child may have include a disability (physical, intellectual, learning), developmental delay, trauma, or chronic illness.

I shared about my daughter Lydia's (and my) struggles with ADHD, as well as her battle with depression and anxiety. It was a rough few years while we first denied, then came to terms with our diagnosis. Once we pursued treatment, while we had reasons to hope, there were times the process was very bleak.

Before the vital turning point of the night Lydia shared her desire to leave the struggle of her life and go to heaven to be with God, I mentioned that she had been a mere shadow of her former happy, joyful, kind, brilliant self for months. Let me tell you what that meant in real talk: She was oppositional, defiant, and raging more often than she was not. Everything was an argument. Every emotion was magnified. Every task was resisted, put off, or refused. She was not self-sufficient to get herself ready in the morning. Homework consumed our lives and my sanity. One afternoon during homework, she passed out as a result of what I now understand to be a panic attack.

She'd rapid-cycle through maniacal bursts of energy and cackling laughter, then she'd crumble into the fetal position crying. She'd have raging tantrums . . . *at ten years old*. Mike and I were very concerned.

She also never slept. I know I said sleep issues are mostly developmental and kids grow out of them. That's true the vast majority of times. It was true for my older, neurotypical daughter. But Lydia didn't sleep through the night even once until she was sixteen months old. Even after she proved she was physically capable of doing so at sixteen months, she rarely slept all night. By the time she was ten, long past when it was developmentally appropriate, she was still getting out of bed multiple times after I'd put her down and waking several times during the night.

On top of those things, Lydia, my husband, and I hadn't slept in *years*. Sleep deprivation was magnifying everything else.

During the months we were dealing with profound behavioral problems with Lydia, we implemented a multipronged strategy of strong boundaries, clearly communicated expectations, consistent consequences for unwanted behavior, a reward system that reinforced desirable behavior, and verbal encouragement for anything we could praise about her. In terms of getting her to sleep, we also tried everything we could think of. All the things the experts said should work, didn't. Like I said, she never got any positive feedback or benefit when she got out of bed, but she continued long past the point that other kids grow out of it. She was desperate for sleep. She wanted it. She'd get in a vicious cycle of worrying that she wouldn't be able to sleep and then be unable to turn off her mind and sleep because she was worried that she wouldn't be able to sleep.[17]

In terms of struggles at school, we tried natural supplements, lists, organizational tools, and training. We even had her start drinking coffee in the mornings. (Caffeine is a home remedy for ADHD because it's a mental stimulant, albeit a weak, unpredictable, and short-acting one. It's perhaps better than nothing, but

---

17   Once treated for ADHD, Lydia gained the capacity to sleep, yet she still needed stress and anxiety management skills as well as sleep hygiene and relaxation skills she'd never developed as a result of her untreated ADHD. A powerful tool we found was a CD called *I Can Relax* by Dr. Donna Pincus. Available on Amazon and iTunes, it's an audio CD teaching relaxation and self-soothing strategies to kids through cognitive-behavioral therapy techniques couched in accessible, kid-friendly stories set to relaxing music. I highly recommend it if you suspect your child's insomnia is fueled by anxiety or an overactive mind or body.

only slightly. It's not a substitute if a doctor has told you your kid needs medication.)

We needed to be doing all of those things. They were the right things. If we had thrown rules, boundaries, and expectations out the window during that time, everything would have been even worse. Failing to reinforce the fact that behavior and choices have consequences wouldn't have been in Lydia's long-term best interest.

But what I hope you see, and what I came to realize, is that all the strategies we were using could only *temporarily* quench Lydia's behavioral fire until we dealt with the accelerant fueling most of Lydia's behavior problems.

Lydia had a legitimate special need—treatment for ADHD—that was not being met. She was trying to get that need met in lots of illegitimate ways. There was plenty of stuff that was chemical, physiological, and psychological that she had no control over. I'm not even talking about behavior that she wasn't really choosing. But amid her mental and emotional chaos, she *was choosing* plenty of words and behavior that were wrong. I believe, on a subconscious level, much of it was a cry for help.

Until we met her ongoing need for ADHD treatment, until we effectively treated and managed her symptoms (her "accelerant"),[18] nothing else we were doing could have a chance to matter.

Before we talk further about special needs, let's acknowledge the elephant in the room. Some people question the legitimacy of mental illness. At the extreme are those who deny that mental illness exists. Less extreme (and perhaps more damaging) are those who believe mental illness exists but is caused by moral failure, bad parenting, laziness, or spiritual weakness.

---

18   Diagnosis, treatment, and effective management of ADHD is a process that takes time, effort, trialing medications, dosages, timing, and counseling. If you are in the midst of this process yourself or with your child, hang in there. The night is darkest before the dawn.

Many Christians tell sufferers to pray harder, trust God more, and perhaps seek deliverance—and then their mental problems will be healed. While I absolutely believe that God can heal us miraculously and that there is a real spiritual battle taking place for our hearts and minds, I categorically reject the notion that all mental illness is primarily the result of spiritual weakness or demonic oppression. To believe that is to thumb our noses at God's design of humans as a perfect blend of body, mind, and spirit. Through God's gift of science, we know that mental illness is *real illness* that deserves diagnosis and treatment just like any other malady.

As Christians, we should offer support to those suffering from mental illness. We should not only pray with and for them, but we should also point them to doctors who can help them. A friend whose child has been diagnosed with bipolar disorder should receive the same concern, compassion, and empathy as if she told you her child has been diagnosed with Type 1 diabetes. We've got to stop feeding the shame cycle that surrounds mental illness because, remember, *shame is never from God.* Believers must help one another take care of our mental health as part of being good stewards of the "temple" of our bodies (1 Corinthians 6:19). The stakes are too high for us to fail at this. Meeting our kids' legitimate special needs means accepting that their special needs may include some form of mental illness.

Maybe you recognize yourself or your child in my family's story. Perhaps it's not ADHD, but a different mental illness. Maybe it's a disability (physical, intellectual, developmental, learning). Maybe it's trauma. When people, especially kids, experience trauma (which can be caused by abuse, neglect, rejection, abandonment, or loss[19]), it changes them temporarily at least, but sometimes permanently.

---

19 Loss can be a move, divorce, death, or any major life change the child perceives as loss.

If you suspect there's an unmet special need at the root of your child's behavior, you must still set clear boundaries, communicate expectations, issue predictable consequences for unwanted choices and behavior, and reward and praise good attributes and actions your kid takes. But until you acknowledge and address your child's unmet special need, everything else is moot.

Until you deal with the source, it's like carefully following a recipe for bread, putting it in the oven, and never turning on the heat. No matter how well you follow the recipe, it will never become bread without a hot oven. On the other hand, turning the oven to the right temperature and leaving the dough in the right amount of time doesn't preclude you from following the recipe. You've still got to discipline, but you've also got to meet their special needs.

I want to point out where this part of the theory breaks down a bit. Some of you might have kids with special needs that you are actively working to meet therapeutically, medically, educationally, and physically. Depending on what type of special need your child has, it might not be something you'll ever be able to fully manage if *manage* means to get it under control to the point where it doesn't precipitate other unwanted behaviors. There are kids with special needs like autism, attachment disorders, intellectual disabilities, and emotional injuries who, even with diligent treatment and therapy, only improve a slight bit or not at all. My heart breaks with you if you're in this place with a special-needs child. I can only encourage you that you're doing God's work. You are giving your all to meet your child's special needs, and that may or may not be enough to affect their behavior. Please don't feel any judgment or shame from me. Feel only my love, empathy, and prayers.

And even if you have been denying, neglecting, or otherwise not actively working to meet a special need your child has (like I ignored Lydia's for so long), also feel no shame. Shame is never from God. Conviction is. Heaviness in your spirit that leads to repentance is. But the God of redemption, grace, forgiveness, and mercy doesn't traffic in shame. Shame is from the enemy. Accept forgiveness, mercy, and grace. Rebuke shame; then move forward. Jesus went to the cross for your freedom.

Finally, if you have a child with special needs, seek support and help. Depending on the special needs you're working with, you might seek out a combination of doctors, mental health professionals, teachers, specialists, counselors, pharmacists, and ministers. Pastors and fellow believers with spiritual gifts in healing, deliverance, and prayer are vital. Yet don't neglect pursuing treatments that come from the gifts of science and medicine that God's designed and ordained as instruments of His healing and restoration here on earth.

Reach out.

Unmet Inner Needs

As we discussed in chapter 2, there are three ongoing inner needs that are universal to every human soul: the need for a secure love, a significant purpose, and a strong hope. As parents, we're the primary earthly relationship God uses to help meet these needs in our kids. The best way we can actively meet these heart needs in our kids is by giving them four key freedoms: the freedom to be different, the freedom to be candid, the freedom to be vulnerable, and the freedom to make mistakes.[20]

---

20   Tim Kimmel, *Grace Based Parenting* (Nashville: Thomas Nelson, 2005), 135.

The three inner needs and the four freedoms are interwoven like a matrix:

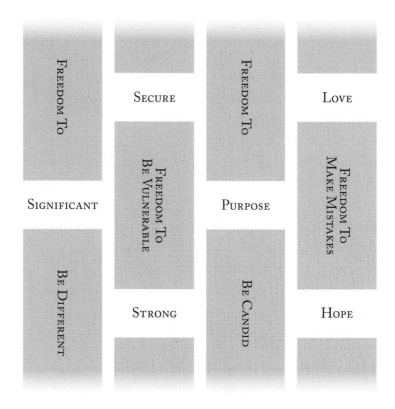

As the graphic illustrates, the needs and freedoms are inter-woven and interdependent like the threads in a tapestry. So, tell me, which thread can I cut and have the weaving continue to hold together? Of course the answer is none of them! No single inner need or freedom is expendable.

Just like the other types of legitimate needs we've identified, sometimes the accelerant fueling our kids' behavior is an unmet or insufficiently met inner need. You might want to pause and consider this if what you're sorting out of your mental basket is an ongoing pattern of behavior like whininess, dishonesty, or defiance. You especially want to stop and analyze if what you're sorting out of your basket is something serious and acute like violence, uncontrollable anger, or sexual experimentation, especially if it's out of character for how your child typically does life.

Is your child hungry for love, purpose, or hope? Maybe they're feeling insecure, insignificant, and weak because they don't feel free to be different, candid, vulnerable, or to make mistakes.

Even when we're making our best attempt to meet their needs by giving them freedom, our kids might not be able to internalize and access the love, purpose, and hope they need because we're speaking a foreign language to them. If their unique personality and strengths reveals that they're from a different "home country" than we are, they might have completely different paradigms for what helps them feel secure, significant, and strong.

For example, if they're a Fun Country kid being forced to live in Perfect Country most of the time, they're going to feel foreign and lost. The same would be true for a kid from Peace Country forced to live in Fun Country, or Control Country forced to dwell in Peace Country, or any other foreign combination.

A Hill to Die On

My daughter Riley's Flag Page assessment reveals that her home country is Perfect Country and her adopted country (scoring second place in her assessment) is Peace Country (the four countries are described on page 46). Her unique design means she is usually kind, responsible, and hardworking. But sometimes her tendencies toward perfectionism drive her to appease others just so she won't have to face conflict.

I picked up Riley from school one afternoon and immediately knew something was wrong. I made subtle hints and then asked her much less subtle questions to try to get to the crux of what was bothering her, but she didn't reveal anything.

I decided to wait. Sure enough, as I was putting her to bed that night, she broke. She told me that day, during their math test, her teacher had to leave to take an urgent phone call. While the teacher was gone, her friend leaned over and told her that she hadn't been able to study because she'd forgotten to bring home her textbook, and she wanted to copy a few answers off Riley's page.

Riley told me she knew it was wrong, but her friend was usually a good student. She didn't want her friend to get a bad grade on the test. She didn't want to lose her friend, so she let her copy as many answers as she could before they heard their teacher's heels click down the hallway.

It was the first time I'd ever faced an instance where one of my girls had cheated. At least as far as I knew, and based on how uncomfortable Riley was acting, I believed it to be the first time. In our family, cheating and dishonesty are felonies. I had to decide what to do. For the moment, I would stall.

I told Riley I was proud of her for having the courage to confess. Being honest about our mistakes and confessing our sins takes courage. *Courage is a big deal in our house.* I also told her that perhaps it was the first time she faced the choice between doing what feels good in the moment and what's right in the long run, but it certainly wouldn't be the last. Life would present her with plenty of opportunities to cheat the system, and she might even watch as people cheating the system seem to get ahead. Even though it seems to work, that doesn't make it prudent. Just because everyone is doing it doesn't make it right. Just because people get away with it doesn't mean it doesn't hurt them or others.

She said she understood, and I asked her to wait a few minutes and I'd be back in to talk to her.

The burning building I'd just walked into was pitch-black. It wasn't safe to take another step until I let my senses focus.

I needed to *stand still*. That's the only way I'd be able to find the source of this fire in the dark.

There was thick smoke obstructing everything. This incident with Riley took place while we were in the thick of untreated ADHD (Lydia's and mine). We were battle weary and preoccupied with fighting Lydia's behavioral fires. Trying to extinguish them produced a noxious smoke that was choking us all.

Riley's choice to cheat on the test could be merely a result of her sin nature. It could also be a reflection of her strengths pushed to an extreme and wanting to please her friend, avoid conflict, and be liked and accepted at any price. Those were all potential motivators. They were in the picture. But they weren't the whole picture.

I knew because we'd been focused on Lydia, because we'd let ADHD consume our home, that Riley was probably suffering from unmet inner needs. In the midst of everything else, she'd lost her sense of security, significance, and strength. Our unintentional neglect had left her hungry for love, purpose, and hope.

Our home was a battlefield and we were falling back. Stress, fatigue, anger, and chaos were unrelenting. Under that kind of oppression, no one felt any sense of freedom to be different, candid, vulnerable, or make mistakes.

Add to that, I'm sure she felt foreign and uncomfortable in the place that was supposed to be her refuge—our home.

Riley's home country is Perfect. Perfection was not a language we spoke. Perfection and ADHD are antithetical. We were so far off that mark, it wasn't funny.

Riley's adopted country is Peace. Peace was not a flag we flew in our home at that point.

If anything, we were living in an extreme and toxic version of *my* adopted country—Control Country—because to battle the chaos, anxiety, anger, and helplessness we were all feeling, I'd started acting like a hypercontrolling dictator. At times, there were no traces of my home country—Fun Country. We couldn't even hear faint echoes of Fun's anthem.

Here's how God designed each member of our family to thrive:

Lydia: Fun/Perfect
Riley: Perfect/Peace
Mike: Peace/Fun
Karis: Fun/Control

Clearly, none of us was at home in our own home. A dictatorial, high-control atmosphere had stripped all of us of our comfort and sense of belonging.[21]

Riley's choice to cheat needed to be dealt with. It wasn't something developmental she'd outgrow or something insignificant we could ignore. It wasn't a time we could be all, "Just whatever." It was a character issue that ten years down the road could cost her too much to let it remain unopposed. She needed correction and consequences.

It *was* a hill worth dying on.

Yet the context of our home mattered. Riley's intentions mattered. Most importantly, we needed to address the unmet inner needs that were fueling her behavior. Otherwise this fire would just pop up somewhere else.

As Mike and I processed everything together, we resolved to fight to regain a sense of freedom in our home and go out of our

---

21   If you are struggling with a toxic, high-control environment or person (especially if that person is you), I recommend Tim Kimmel, *The High Cost of High Control: How to Deal with Powerful Personalities* (Scottsdale, AZ: Family Matters, 2005).

way to affirm Riley, to make sure she felt loved by us and God, to reframe the vision of our God-given purpose as a family and as individuals, and to remember in Whom we find our hope.

If we didn't, the grace-based consequences Mike and I were planning to enforce would come up short.

chapter seven

GIVE APPROPRIATE CONSEQUENCES

For the moment all discipline seems painful rather than pleasant, but later it yields the peaceful fruit of righteousness to those who have been trained by it.
—Hebrews 12:11

My dad used to say, "Never drive in a thumbtack with a sledgehammer. You'll only end up with a huge hole in the wall."

I finally understand the metaphor.

When our kids break the rules (and they will), we must correct them. It's important, though, that our correction is proportionate to their behavior.

- If we overreact and use a sledgehammer on a thumbtack, it does more harm to the wall than anything else.
- If we underrespond and try to use a tack hammer to drive a masonry nail into a brick wall, we might break our hammer, or our hand . . . or both. And the effort will be for nothing because we've made no progress.

In both extremes, choosing the wrong-sized hammer for the job erodes the trust that's essential to our grace-based discipline having its intended effect. It also causes reckless and unnecessary damage.

Properly Sized Hammers

I was thinking a lot about hammers and nails after Riley confessed to cheating on the test. I needed to choose the proper hammer. I didn't know what to do.

My husband knows a whole lot more about hammers than I do. Providentially, he was hanging out in the land of hammers, the garage, so I decided to go talk to him. I described the job: Riley's choice was both a violation of integrity (character) and out of character from the way she usually lived.

Yet we had to consider the context of the last few months. In our family's weary battle with ADHD, we'd let Riley become hungry for her core inner needs for love, purpose, and hope.

Also, Riley seemed contrite and her choice had clearly been killing her until she confessed.

"Is that enough?" I asked Mike. "Do I even *need* a hammer?"

Wisely, the hammer expert said, "Let's pray."

Problem or Opportunity?

After we prayed, we both felt that while it was certainly a problem, it was also an opportunity for us to have a strong influence on whether or not Riley would ever cheat again. This might have been the first time, but we also wanted it to be the last.

We went in to talk to Riley.

We could tell she was sorry. We were proud of her for confessing, but this wasn't over yet.

Sure, her own conscience stung—but sometimes to heal a wound, you've got to wash it with something that stings *even worse* to make sure it doesn't fester. It brought us no joy to cause her more pain, but this wasn't about our comfort. It was about her healing.

Because we love Riley, we needed her to remember that *cheating causes pain* and *choices have a price.*

Discipline, Not Punishment

I'm not sure if you've noticed, but I haven't used the word *punishment* in this book until now. That's been intentional. Most people understand *discipline* and *punishment* to be synonyms, but there's an important distinction between the two.

Punishment is retaliatory. It's payback. It's about avenging the victim and appeasing society's hunger for justice by letting them watch the offender get what they deserve.

Punishment is done primarily for the victim's sake, to avenge the crimes committed against them and send the message that anyone who offends society will pay. Offenders are punished to protect society and prevent more people from becoming victims.

Discipline is different. It doesn't share the same purpose as punishment. When you think about it, it has the *complete opposite purpose.* Punishment and discipline aren't synonyms; they're antonyms.

Discipline isn't about avenging the victim. It's about doing what's best for the one who did the victimizing. Discipline is done for the sake of the offender. It's done to redirect them back within the boundaries that will ensure their safety and increase their joy.

Discipline corrects to reform behavior that society will punish in order to ultimately spare the offender from further suffering under the gavel of justice. Offenders are disciplined to protect them from future pain.

Punishment is motivated by vengeance.

Discipline is motivated by love.

Grace-based parents never punish their kids; they discipline. I know that because God never punishes us, at least not anymore.

In the kingdom of God, punishment no longer exists. Punishment was banished when Jesus went to the cross. When He died, He was punished for the sins of the world. The Bible says, "He was pierced for our transgressions, he was crushed for our iniquities; the punishment that brought us peace was on him, and by his wounds we are healed" (Isaiah 53:5 NIV).

In the verse above, notice the phrase "the punishment that brought us peace." I believe that's the peace of knowing our punishment was banished along with our sin.

Then Isaiah says, "By his wounds we are healed." Jesus's sacrifice brought healing of our preexisting heart condition. The cure for our sin. A resurrection out of our constant death.

Jesus's death on the cross was the end of punishment for the children of God. "Therefore, there is now no condemnation for those who are in Christ Jesus" (Romans 8:1 NIV). We who are in Christ Jesus are no longer condemned to die for our sins or be punished for our unrighteousness. And "now no condemnation" means exactly that . . . from now on, none. No condemnation. Never again.

The key, though, is that this truth applies only to those who have given themselves over to Christ, who have submitted their will and repented of their sins. We are then no longer subject to the penalties of the old law that says sin is punished by our own death (Romans 6:23). We've been given citizenship to a new kingdom with a new law: grace. No more punishment. No more condemnation.

If you've put your faith in Christ, then you're one of God's children. God never punishes His children, and we shouldn't punish ours. Like God, we need to discipline them with grace instead.

The Purpose of Pain

Discipline and punishment have something in common, which may explain why we assume they're the same:

Pain.

Punishment inflicts pain . . . and sometimes so does discipline. The difference, and this is key, is the purpose that pain serves in either case.

In punishment, *the purpose of pain is to satisfy justice*, to see the offender experience at least as much pain as he inflicted on the victims. *Punishment uses pain to enact vengeance.*

In discipline, *the purpose of pain is to ensure joy*, to correct the offender's behavior in order to protect him from further pain. *Discipline uses pain to express love.*

Parents, we must make our peace with pain. We cannot administer grace-based discipline without it.

When our kids do stuff we know isn't in their long-term best interest, whether their behavior is sinful or simply won't lead them down the path where they'll experience the most joy, we need to *discipline them.* And sometimes that will mean *painful consequences*, whether imposed or natural.

- When we discipline, it means sometimes we (or another authority figure) impose painful consequences in order to correct our kids out of love.

- It might also mean we allow natural consequences to teach our children, and natural consequences are oftentimes painful.

Part of love is overcoming our primal instinct to shield our kids from all pain now in order to correct behavior that, if continued, will hurt even worse and cost even more later.

Pain is a powerful motivator. It causes us to quickly stop whatever we were doing when we feel it and avoid the place the pain occurred. For good or bad, we typically choose our behavior to avoid pain. Our kids are more likely to avoid things that cause them pain and stop doing things that hurt.

And I'm not just talking about physical pain but emotional pain as well.

As parents, seeing our kids get hurt hurts us. Our kids' pain is our pain. That's why intentionally imposing or allowing painful consequences requires sacrifice on our part. It means consciously choosing pain. But we do it because we can look into the future and see how a little pain now avoids a lot of pain later. And ultimately, that's better for our kids.

Love is the only motivator more powerful than pain. And love is what we need to focus on when we discipline with grace.

The Cost of Choices

Punishment and discipline have not only pain in common but also cost. Both punishment and discipline *attach a price* to wrong behavior.

Punishment seeks restitution to the victim by requiring the offender to pay. It might be a monetary fine, a debt to society repaid through incarceration or community service, or even a stolen life repaid with an execution.

Punishment attaches a price to behavior and requires repayment of that debt in order to get justice for the victim.

Discipline is different.

A price is still attached to behavior, and payment of that penalty is still sought, but only because requiring the offender to give up something he values causes him a certain level of pain, and discipline uses pain for the offender's good, to teach and reform him.

Also, discipline requires repayment because it involves the offender in the restoration process and gives him or her the opportunity to experience redemption. *Discipline charges a price to restore the offender and redeem his or her future.*

Discipline Does Not Use Shame

Because we're imperfect human parents, we often go off the safe path as we travel the dusty road of parenting. We need signposts to direct us and fences to protect us from crossing out of bounds and potentially off a cliff.

Both punishment and discipline have pain and cost in common, but discipline uses both for redemptive purposes. These distinctions are your signposts, but I also need to point out a fence I had put in because I've seen far too many parents go off the trail and slide down a dangerous embankment into shame.

Discipline doesn't ever use shame. As you are learning to discipline with grace—and while you are trying to choose appropriate, effective responses to correct your child's behavior—always be mindful that shame and humiliation are incompatible with grace-based discipline.

Now, I'm not talking about a little innocent embarrassment. I have tweens and teens. A bit of good-natured teasing, busting some sweet dance moves in front of their friends, and hugging and kissing them in public are all frequently part of my repertoire. Embarrassing my kids is my favorite sport. I'm training for the Olympics.

Shame and humiliation are different. Shame and humiliation seek to wound, to oppress. They are methods of toxic high control. Shame and humiliation are never from God; they are only from the enemy. When God disciplines us, He never uses shame and humiliation as tools. Therefore, shame and humiliation have no place in a grace-based parent's strategy for discipline.

Here are some examples: verbally berating her in front of her peers, making a kid pull down his pants for a spanking, name-calling, bringing up their mistakes over and over again, or publicly shaming them on Facebook or other social media.

So, to keep us all away from the dangerous ditch, when you're choosing and administering discipline, ask yourself: *Is this humiliating for my kid? Am I using shame to correct?*

It doesn't matter if you're spanking them, putting them in time-out, or taking away a privilege; once you couple those legitimate forms of discipline with shame and humiliation, they become illegitimate. They go from being tools to being weapons depending on how they're used.

What Are Consequences?

Consequences are uncomfortable or undesirable outcomes of behavior. Consequences can be seen as the cost of our behavior and also the pain that that price or outcome inflicts.

Remember that in grace-based discipline:

- the role of pain is to reform the offender and ensure their ultimate joy;
- the offender pays a price to bring about their own restoration and redeem their future.

How do we choose consequences? How do we choose the right-sized hammer for the job we need to do? How do we apply just enough pain now to protect our kids from far more pain later? How do we know what price to attach to wrong behavior?

All consequences involve some type of pain (physical, emotional, and psychological) and/or some amount of cost. And the younger your child is, the shorter your time window is for an effective response. This is just developmental. A young child's developing brain simply cannot connect a consequence to a behavior that happened too far in the past. A toddler needs an almost immediate response to associate an unwanted behavior with an undesirable consequence.

As kids grow, as their brains grow, your window of response grows with them.

As parents, choosing and applying consequences carefully and consistently is one of the most loving things we can do because it protects our kids from far worse consequences later.

Yet imposing or allowing consequences is inherently hard because it means overcoming our natural instinct to avoid pain. Because our kids' pain is our pain, when we impose or allow painful, costly consequences to shape our child's behavior, we choose to enter into pain ourselves. This is where we need to remember that discipline is motivated by love, and love is the only motivator powerful enough to overcome our natural desire to avoid pain.

Imposed Consequences

Imposed consequences are chosen and applied by us or another trusted authority figure. Time-outs, loss of privileges, chores, removal of possessions, isolation from activities or social interactions, retraction of independence, fines, and spanking[22] are all examples of imposed consequences.

Whenever possible warn your kids of consequences in advance. But remember, if you promise a consequence, *always* follow through. That's why you should only promise consequences you are willing and able to follow through on.

---

22   For a more in-depth discussion of spanking, see Appendix B.

For example, you might say, "The next time you throw that block, you will get a spanking." (And when he does, he gets a spanking.)

Do not say: "If you leave your toys in the hallway again, I am going to throw them all in the trash" unless you will actually do it. (I, personally, don't love throwing away things that I purchased with my hard-earned money for my kids, so I'd have a hard time following through if I threatened this.)

Do not say: "If you sass me again, no TV for a month" unless you're willing to withhold TV for a month. (I would find it near impossible because I like to watch TV with my kids.)

Consequences Imposed by Others

When our kids are under our roof, it's mostly us, their parents, imposing the consequences. We have the opportunity to partner, though, with a team of allies—trusted authority figures who can add an extra layer of accountability and reinforcement to our efforts. For you, this might be your kids' grandparents, aunts, and uncles. Or it might be members of your community like teachers, principals, or police officers.

Don't undermine consequences given to your kid by a trusted authority figure like a grandparent or their teacher. Don't bail your kids out of everything.

For example, if your child gets caught cheating in school, don't protest when the teacher gives her a zero on the quiz. Or if the principal calls and says your nine-year-old son threw sand at another boy again after two warnings, let the principal keep your son in the office and let him "sweat" a little, then do community service for the next three days during recess.

Cultivating trusting relationships with these other authority figures, and then recognizing and deferring to their authority, prepares your kid for adult life where they will need to respect the authority of people like their bosses.

Natural Consequences

Because we're smart people and we have a firm grasp on the obvious, I don't have to explain the natural consequences of gravity, inertia, or thermodynamics. I don't need to tell you that what goes up comes down, that inertia can have a damaging effect on our skulls, or that stoves are often hotter than our skin is designed to handle. Yet if you've ever been to a monster truck rally you might question the assumption that these natural forces are common knowledge.

I also don't need to remind you that bodies function poorly and get fat on a diet of Doritos and chocolate chip cookies or that muscles atrophy when all they do is push buttons on a remote control. We know these things. But based on my own nutritional intake of coffee, grilled cheese sandwiches, and diet cranberry juice and my daily exercise routine of walking from my office to the break room refrigerator and back, you might question whether I have any business blabbering to you about natural consequences.

That's the thing about natural consequences, though. Whether we acknowledge them or not, natural consequences exist. Denying or ignoring them doesn't make them less real. These are results that simply happen and there's not always anything we can do about it. Also, natural consequences are often the most painful. They are painful not only physically but also emotionally and psychologically.

For example, you tell your son, "Don't run by the pool!" After you remind him for the fourth time, he finally slips, falls on his face, and bites his lip—experiencing a painful natural consequence.

Or you warn your daughter that exaggerating stories about where she's traveled or people she's met to impress her classmates isn't honest or authentic. Eventually, people will lose trust in her and not want to be her friend anymore. She continues. They don't trust her. She gets ostracized.

There are subtler types of natural consequences that might not always be obvious. Relationally, we lose trust in someone who routinely fails to follow through on their promises. Financially, we become enslaved to debt and miss out on future opportunities when we spend more money than we have.

It's *sometimes possible* for us to block or bail our kids out of certain natural consequences. Even when we can't completely deflect them, we sometimes try to partially shield our kids.

I don't know your story or situation, but I do know that the best time to let our kids learn hard lessons from natural consequences is while they are young and in our care. Natural consequences are often harsh and indiscriminate. In our home, our kids have the benefit of our comfort and support. As kids, they have the advantage of time to recover and change.

The more we allow our kids to feel the full brunt of natural consequences and help them learn from them while they are still in our homes, the more pain we prevent them from experiencing as a result of natural consequences in the future.

What Is Your Kids' Currency?

In order for a consequence to cost them something, in order for it to be uncomfortable and undesirable enough to affect their future behavior and choices, our kids need to pay for their actions in the currency they value.

For example, don't give your strong-willed four-year-old a withering stare and sigh when he defies you. *He doesn't care about your withering stare.* He's like Rocky Balboa saying, "Is that all you got?" Your frustrated sigh feels good to him. He pins it to his chest like a merit badge.

Or after a particularly dreadful stint in the doctor's waiting room, telling your two-year-old, "Shredding all those magazines was a very bad choice and now you can't go to the park with your friend Emma on Thursday" is about as effective as discussing Russian literature with your parakeet. Two-year-olds don't have a social life. Time with their friends is not their currency. They're not thinking about Thursday. They don't even understand the concept of time . . . or friends!

Or if you threaten to spank your seventeen-year-old for violating their curfew, they'd probably be like, "Go ahead! It won't hurt, it's over fast, and then I can get back to my important social life!"

Regardless of developmental stage, our kids' unique personalities—or "home countries" (see page 46)—add nuance to what they value every step of the way.

Developmental Currency

Your kids' currency tends to follow a predictable pattern that not only tracks with their "home country" but also with their developmental stage.[23]

Toddlers—1.5 to 3.5 Years

Toddlers' currency is *having*. In particular, their currency is having or possessing objects. Even more specifically, possessing objects they can see, right now, in the moment.

---

23   My developmental currency theory is an amalgamation of the conclusions of several other psychological theories, including Piaget's Stage Theory, Massey's Moral Development Theory, and Devito's Relationship Stages Theory. The test I applied to all conclusions was, "Does this make common sense?"

Brain development dictates that children in this stage understand only tangibles. They don't value or understand intangibles like time, doing activities, and friendship. Also, toddlers have a warped idea of ownership and therefore what they feel they're entitled to possess: if they can see it and they want it, it belongs to them.

That's why your two-year-old sees the ball her brother is playing with; points at it; says, "Mine!"; and then runs over and swipes it out of his hands. Toddlers frequently use the word *mine* for any object they can see.

Examples of consequences that act on toddlers' primary currency (having) are removing desired object from child; removing child from desired object, room, person, or anything they are trying to possess; or straightforward physical discipline like spanking[24] or swatting a hand.

Preschoolers—3.5 to 5 Years

Preschoolers' currency is *doing*. This new currency doesn't mean kids abandon their first currency of having objects, but they also start to value time doing pleasurable activities.

Brain development is starting to grasp intangibles like activities and time. They start to value time doing an activity they like (coloring, running, swimming, eating). Also, around this time preschoolers start to enjoy interacting with their peers, but only when it means doing things they like. A group of preschool-aged boys might play and interact over a tower of blocks, but as soon as something else they would rather do or an object they would rather possess becomes available, they'll abandon their playmates without a second thought.

Examples of consequences that act on preschoolers' primary currency (doing) are removing the child from the activity they

---

24   For a more thorough discussion of spanking, see Appendix B.

are enjoying at the time, isolating the child for a time-out, or straightforward physical discipline like spanking or swatting a hand.

School-Aged Children—5.5 to 8 Years

School-age children's currency is *being*. At this stage, kids start to place more value on relationships. This is when it starts to matter less what they're in possession of or what activity they're doing and more who they're with.

School-age kids start forming meaningful bonds with peers, and being present in those relationships becomes a goal. They still value objects and activities but are willing to compromise those currencies at times if it means more access to the relationships they value.

Examples of consequences that act on school-aged children's primary currency (being) are removing an object from their possession or stalling an activity that they want to do, especially objects and activities that they prioritize because they perceive those objects and activities as ways that they are able to be with people/friends they value; isolating them from people they want to be with; or removing ongoing or future privileges (more commonly known as "grounding").

Tweens—8.5 to 12 Years

Tweens' currency is *belonging*. For tweens, the value they place on being with people they like grows and morphs to take on an even deeper meaning. They don't just want to be with their friends; they want to belong.

In order to belong, tweens feel a deep need to fit in, or at least not stand out too much. At the time in their lives when they are the most physically and socially awkward, they are also the most concerned that they don't appear weird. The irony! The tension!

For tweens, possessing objects and doing activities are valued but only as a means to belong. Ultimately, what tweens value most is belonging in meaningful relationships with their peer group and their friends.

Examples of consequences that act on tweens' primary currency (belonging) are "grounding," removal of valued objects/activities, and repayment of damages (can be paid back with money, time, labor, or other creative exchanges).

Teens—13 to 18 Years

Teens' currency is *independence*. Having desirable possessions, doing enjoyable activities, being with their friends, and belonging to a meaningful group in their overall social structure are still valuable currencies, but independence starts to float to the top.[25]

Teens want to think independent thoughts, have independent opinions, and have independent time, possessions, relationships, and purpose. Independence from what, you ask? From us, their parents. Y'all, we are the oppressors! And they cry, "Freedom!" To teens, independence from us, their parents, whether they consciously understand or express it, is the primary motivation behind nearly everything they do. And it's an important developmental step toward the goal of successful adult life. But, as you may or may not recall from your own teenage years, teens don't have a fully developed prefrontal cortex, the part of the brain responsible for executive functions like impulse control, planning, strategy, risk assessment, emotional regulation, and working memory.

So basically, they lack *wisdom*. Teens want freedom but don't

---

25   You might wonder about *actual currency*—money. Once kids can grasp the concept (around age three or four), they start to value money, but only because it's something they can exchange for their developmental currency. Namely, they trade money for having, doing, being, belonging, and independence.

always have the wisdom to use it wisely. They are Ferraris with golf-cart brakes. Sometimes teens are willing to sacrifice lesser currencies like possessions and activities, and even do things they don't really want to do, in order to be in relationships with people they value and therefore *belong* (independently, of course). Add to that, their hormones make them walking chemical warheads.

Examples of consequences that act on teens' primary currency (independence) include grounding, restricting curfew, removing valued objects and activities such as cell phones or cars/driving, or demanding repayment for damages with money, labor, or other creative exchanges.

The facts that teenagers are fiercely independent and have underdeveloped wisdom but also hormone-fueled energy and supercharged emotions are true. But they are not the whole truth.

Based on that description, it might surprise you that *teenagers are my favorite!* They're fun, smart, interesting, brave, emotional, creative, inventive, loving, and empathetic, and you guys, sometimes they let me hang out with them!

Redemptive Prophesies

I don't care what you've heard—we can choose to categorically reject the prophecy that teenagers become dreadful nightmares. (And really, we can do this at any phase.) Instead, we can adopt a more redemptive narrative about them well in advance, until that new narrative becomes truth. When our kids hear us say with confidence that their teen years are going to be the best ever, and that they're going to be the smartest, bravest, most creative, innovative, inclusive, empathetic, loving, transformational generation the world has ever seen, there's at least a chance they might believe it and start living like it's true!

And when you spend the early years laying the groundwork

by parenting and disciplining with grace, you set your kids on a trajectory to become teens whose great qualities far outweigh their flaws.

I'll admit, some days it will seem as though your teenagers wake up as porcupines, but they still need to know that they're *our* porcupines, and we aren't afraid to love them.

You might think I'm just naturally optimistic or filled with blind faith, but that'd be too generous. I only know this is possible because it's what my parents did for my siblings and me. I only know it's reality because it's the reality that grace-based parenting brought about in our home.

Time for Consequences

Remember when I told you that Riley confessed to cheating on her math test? It was time for sentencing.

For Riley, we decided she needed to confess to her teacher that she had cheated and be willing to accept any consequences her teacher would dish out. We explained that might include both her and her friend receiving zeroes on their tests because there was no way to tell her teacher she'd let her classmate copy without the teacher knowing who it was. Her friend might be really angry with her for turning them both in.

But sometimes the result of one bad choice is very hard consequences.

We hoped next time someone asked to copy off of her, she'd realize it's easier and less painful to say no in the moment than deal with the consequences later.

I told her I'd take her to talk with her teacher and stay by her side the whole time if she wanted. I sent her teacher an e-mail that night saying we'd like to come by fifteen minutes before class to speak with her.

Morning came and Riley was up and dressed before her alarm went off. She had a hint of the look I imagine a death-row inmate has on the day of his execution. For Riley, a kid from Perfect/Peace Country, having to admit to wrongdoing, especially to her teacher whose approval she values, was almost the worst consequence she could imagine. Almost.

Confessing was also going to mean turning in her friend and potentially earning them both zeroes on their tests. A zero is as far from perfect as it gets. Disappointing her teacher and embarrassing her friend were not the peaceful outcomes she sought in her relationships.

Riley knew this was the right thing, but she was dreading it so much she couldn't eat breakfast. She just wanted to get it over with.

The time finally came. We walked into her otherwise empty classroom, and she tearfully confessed to her teacher that she'd let her friend copy off her paper during the test. She was sorry. She knew it was wrong but she did it anyway. She gained control of her quivering lip and said she'd accept whatever consequences her teacher felt were fair.

Her teacher let the silence hang about as long as the three of us could bear.

She told Riley that cheating *was indeed* wrong... that cheating as an adult can result in losing a job or a spouse and can even mean going to prison.

Riley's eyes got wide and she drew in a sharp breath.

Her teacher (who endeared herself to me more and more over the course of her tenure) said *this time*, she thought having to confess was enough. She knew it had to be hard for Riley. She knew how worried Riley probably was about what her friend would think.

Her teacher said Riley was a good student, an honest person who, as far as she knew, had never done anything like this before. She wasn't going to give them zeroes this time, but if she ever heard about Riley doing anything like this again, she'd make sure the consequences were doubled. She'd "testify for the prosecution" if she had to.

This teacher was a serious woman, and we knew she meant it.

Her teacher stood, gathered Riley up in a rare hug, caught my eye and gave me the slightest wink, then ushered us out of the room.

chapter eight

MORE THAN CONSEQUENCES

It is for discipline that you have to endure.
God is treating you as sons. For what son
is there whom his father does not disci-
pline? If you are left without discipline, in
which all have participated, then you are
illegitimate children and not sons. Besides
this, we have had earthly fathers who dis-
ciplined us and we respected them. Shall
we not much more be subject to the Father
of spirits and live?
—Hebrews 12:7–9

Over the course of our marriage, Mike and I have always had dogs. Actually, I adopted our first dog while we were engaged, even though we were living separately. I called Mike one afternoon to tell him I was going to the shelter to look at some dogs, so did he want to come with me? He was too young and naive to realize that in female code "look" meant *get* and "did he want to come with me" meant *this is your only chance to object, so take it or leave it.*

I fell in love with a gorgeous one-year-old Dalmatian named Ivan, filled out the paperwork, paid the adoption fee, and that was that. Our dog needed to stay at the shelter to finish his vaccines and get neutered. He'd be ready to come home in four days.

But I was scheduled to be out of town in four days, so I called Mike to let him know when our dog would be ready to come home and see if he could pick him up while I was gone.

"Our dog? You said you were going to *look!*" he said.

"I *did* look. I looked, I loved, we have a dog, so can you pick him up on Thursday?" I said. "It's only three months till the wedding, and my apartment's too small for him anyway. Your house is about to be our house and Ivan's forever home. Why move him twice?"

I heard him sigh loudly into the receiver. And then he said, "Okay."

That's how we got our first dog, and we've had dogs ever since: two different Dalmatians, a German shepherd-like mutt, and now Linkyn, our Chihuahua mix puppy and Mabel, our Jack Russell mix with the Troll Doll hair.[26]

With all our dogs we struggled against the same behavior problem: bolting out the front door.

It seemed as though their life goal was to free themselves from endless treats and comfy couches to taste the wide-open concrete wilderness beyond our front door. They would get out, we'd chase them and finally catch them, bring them over to the door, scold them, swat their nose, and they'd cower and look sorry.

We hoped they'd learned their lesson.

If you know anything about dogs (we clearly didn't), you know that the dogs hadn't learned anything other than (a) bolting out the front door is fun, (b) all the humans chase you, and (c) you

26 Mabel is a mutt. We can only guess at her lineage. She looks like a Jack Russell mixed with something like a Maltese or Shitzu. I'd rather imagine that she is the unlikely love-child of a Jack Russell terrier and a Troll Doll toy because her hair, especially the hair directly on top of her head, is the exact texture of a Troll Doll's.

get lots of attention and then go home and drink from the toilet. The front door was a constant battle. We were always fearful they'd run. So we'd hold them back and block them in an effort to get them *not to do the thing they shouldn't do*—bolt.

When we got Mabel, a friend introduced us to a dog trainer. When the trainer asked us what our biggest goal was, we said, "We just want our kids, their friends, and our guests to be able to come in and out the door and not have to worry that the dog is going to bolt and lead us on a thirty-minute chase, or worse, get hit by a car."

She asked us what we'd done about this problem in the past. We told her about our scolding and swatting and holding back and blocking.

"Have you tried teaching her what she's *supposed* to do by the door instead?"

"No," we said. We didn't want our dog to do anything by the door. We wanted her not to bolt out. We wanted to be able to open the door and have her do nothing.

"Dogs can't do *nothing*," the trainer said. "They don't have that ability. They can only do *something*. Fortunately, they can only do one *something* at a time, so if they're doing something you *don't* want them to do, you've got to teach them something you want them to do instead. And practice that something a lot. Praise and reward it a lot. Reward it so much they *can't wait* to do that something the next time."

She recommended we teach Mabel to sit on a mat directly by the front door. We'd carry her over and set her on her mat, praise her, and give her a treat. Soon, we could say, "Go to your spot!" and she'd run over and sit on her mat. We kept a package of treats on a shelf above her spot, and every time we saw her there, we gave her a treat. Then we started asking her to go there every time we went out, and we'd praise her and give her a treat. Anytime we came in the door we'd ask her to sit on her mat, and we'd give her a treat. (Are you catching a pattern? So did Mabel.)

Finally, we started asking her to sit when someone else came to the door. I'd have the neighbor ring the doorbell and ask Mabel to sit on her mat. I'd open the door and let the neighbor in, tell Mabel to stay, and give her a treat.

Now if Mabel hears a doorbell on TV, if a car drives by outside, or if there's any noise that even remotely sounds like a knock or the door opening, she runs to her mat, sits, and looks at me expectantly. I always try to praise her. She doesn't always get a treat, but now, I honestly think she just likes knowing what she's supposed to do.

Mabel feels at peace knowing how she's supposed to behave instead. And now that she knows what she's supposed to do at the door, she's never once tried to bolt.

Unlike dogs, kids are moral beings with complex psyches. Also, kids are (usually) more intelligent. Yet there's a common thread: *kids don't have the ability to do nothing either.* If all we ever do is correct and dish out consequences, then all we ever say is no, don't do, don't say, don't go, *don't bolt out that door.*

We constantly live in the negative. We feel it, and our kids feel it.

On the other hand, there's almost always an opportunity to teach our kids a positive *something* they can do instead. Teaching our kids actions, words, and behavior to use instead of what we don't want them to do gives them opportunities to redirect their focus toward behavior we can praise, affirm, and reward. It frees our kids and us from always feeling negative and creates a positive, grace-based environment.

Grace-Based Discipline: A Multilayer Strategy

Grace-based discipline, discipline that is *for* our kids, is more than just consequences for their actions. It's multilayered and multifaceted. It includes consequences, but it involves a lot more than that.

It's a recipe requiring:

- a thermostat set on grace (and avoiding the extreme temperatures of either legalism or license); well-maintained relationships that actively seek to meet one another's inner needs (secure love, significant purpose, strong hope) by granting the people we love freedom to be different, candid, vulnerable, and make mistakes;
- clear, fair, and gracious rules, regulations, and boundaries that exist primarily for your child's best interest and eventual joy;
- relating to your kids in a way that recognizes and celebrates their unique design (their home country, stage of development, motivations, special needs);
- separating our child's behavior from his or her heart in order to see our child more as God does;
- prioritizing and rightly judging stuff we process out of our mental basket;
- discerning the difference between behavior requiring discipline and behavior that simply bothers us; and
- careful consideration of context and motives behind our kids' behavior so we don't end up treating only symptoms and neglecting to treat the true disease.

Once we've determined which behavior warrants our response, we can carefully formulate a multipronged strategy to discipline our children holistically, appropriately, and effectively.

Looking at this recipe for grace-based discipline with all of its ingredients might make you wonder how you're going to remember all these things . . . especially in the highly dramatic moment of disobedience! I'll admit there are a lot of dynamics to consider as you decide how and when to discipline, but I promise that you get better with practice.

Think back to when you were first learning to drive a car. When you got behind the wheel, there seemed to be a million things to remember—adjust the seat, put your seat belt on, put your foot on the brake, start the car, release the emergency brake, adjust the mirror, look both ways . . . it's a miracle any of us learned to drive and did it safely. But now that I've been driving for twenty years, I take off and go from point A to point B with hardly a thought. Sometimes I can't even remember the trip—yikes!

It's the same with grace-based discipline. It will become a logical flow of thoughts and decisions that you'll make as you go from the offense to the consequence. A lot of times you won't even be able to pinpoint how you got there, but you'll have disciplined with grace.

Congratulations Are in Order

Before we move on, I think congratulations are in order. You have graduated from both Grace-Based Discipline 101 and 202! Little by little throughout this book, you have learned how to put your natural reactions on hold in order to become a more responsive parent when it comes to discipline. What follows is the 303-level course. It's here that we start to really drill down into specific tactics that you can put in your repertoire now that you understand the philosophy and strategies that govern grace-based, responsive parenting. Fair warning: we're about to blast through a ton of information. And unless you'd like this book to be the length of a Victor Hugo novel, I'm just going to have to state stuff plainly and leave it at that. If you notice a change in my tone, it's because I'm trying desperately to keep a straight face so that I can put all this important information into your capable hands. There are jokes and winding narratives that are trying to get me to crack a smile and disrupt the firehose-flow of this information, but *ain't nobody got time for that!*

Discipline Tactics: A Menu

As grace-based parents, our strategy for discipline needs to be tailored to our kids. We need to take context, motivations, and our kids' own unique design into account for our discipline to be effective. Also, grace-based discipline is more than just dishing out consequences but an opportunity to encourage, train, and prepare our kids as well.

When it's time to respond to a behavior problem with our kids, we have a menu of choices. Except it's more like a sushi menu. We don't have to pick just one. Because discipline is more than merely consequences and requires a multilayered approach; and because we need to customize our response differently each time and with each kid, it helps to know we can combine menu items, simply order one, or order them all at the same time. And these items on the sushi menu tend to *enhance* one another.

Use the menu on the next page as a quick reference to remind yourself of all your options:[27]

---

27   This list is not exhaustive. It is simply my attempt to give you a broad and diverse menu of choices.

Sushi Menu
Discipline Tactics

☐ Tag Behavior*

☐ Pardon

☐ Ignore

☐ Teach

☐ Distract

☐ Re-Direct

☐ (use) Positive Reinforcement

☐ Encourage

☐ (give) Do-Overs

☐ Engineer their Environment for Success

*If you don't know what else to do,
or don't think you should do anything else, always tag behavior.

All menu items compliment and enhance each other.
Order one, or many!

Tag Behavior

Call the behavior what it is. Call it a lie, a cheat, a broken promise, or an unkind word. It's important that we tag wrong or inappropriate behavior, even if we don't do anything else. We do that by verbally acknowledging it, at the very least. If you're only going to order one thing off the sushi menu, this is it. Here is why.

For young kids whose brain development makes it harder for them to connect a consequence to a negative behavior if too much time has passed, tagging the behavior immediately seals the event in their mind and buys you a little time to take them to another room or a private place to administer a consequence.

Even in times you give complete mercy, it's still important to acknowledge wrong behavior.

A note of caution: make sure to choose words that label the behavior and not your child. For example, if your child lies to you say, "That was a lie," or, "What you just said isn't true." Don't say, "You are a liar."

If your child is bullying their younger sibling say, "That's bullying," or, "That was unkind." Don't say, "You're a bully."

Our words have power, especially the words we speak over our children. Their behavior determines what they do; it doesn't have to define who they are. In fact, when we're careful to tag behavior without labeling our kids, the unspoken message is, "What you did was wrong but I believe you are more than that!"

Pardon

Sometimes we recognize that the guilt our kids feel as a result of what they did is penalty enough and we see that mercy and forgiveness are what's in their best interest so that shame doesn't take root in their hearts. We can choose to issue a pardon.

Jesus pardoned the woman caught in adultery (John 8:3–11). He determined that what was best for her, and what would win and transform her heart, was mercy, a full pardon. Yet He still tagged her behavior when He said, "Go, and from now on sin no more" (v. 11).

Ignore

At times you can choose to completely ignore your kids' behavior. Of course, don't do this when it's dangerous behavior. When you are dealing with actions or choices that endanger your child or someone else, whether that danger is physical, spiritual, or emotional, you don't have the option to ignore. Also, if it's a character issue or a choice that'll cost your kids if they continue to do it later in life, you really shouldn't ignore it.

But there's plenty of stuff, especially behavior your kids do primarily to get a rise out of you, that when ignored, will shrivel and die much faster. Some kids use words and actions as bait to engage you in battle and wear you out. They don't always know why they do this. Sometimes it's a subconscious reach for attention, *any attention*, they can glean from you even if it's negative. In that case, when you engage your kids' unwanted behavior, even if it's with pushback, you're actually reinforcing it. We did this when we fought and pulled back on our dog's collar as Mabel tried to bolt out the door. It wasn't a pat on the head or a kind word, but it was contact and attention and it reinforced, rather than deterred, our dog's struggle to get out the door.

Teach

One of our most sacred roles as parents is to teach. Life provides many opportunities to help our kids learn from their mistakes, and a key part of doing that is making sure they have the skills to behave differently in the future. If we determine that they are lacking these skills, then we need to be intentional to build or strengthen basic skills and character where they're deficient.

Teach basic skills

Basic skills include taking turns, table manners, personal hygiene, time management, organization that works for them, social skills, and money management. When we notice patterns in our kids' behavior, it might be because we need to teach our kids basic skills.

Here's a question from a mom whose son needed more help with basic skills:

> Jack struggles to get ready independently in the morning. Mornings are frantic, frustrating, and I end up running around at the last minute doing stuff for him he should be able to do himself. I just assumed this was normal, that I'd need to remind him of every step, every morning until who-knows-when ... maybe he was still too young. I posted about it on Facebook, and my friends chimed in to tell me that no, an eight-year-old boy should be capable to get himself ready. Now I feel like a failure and I'm resenting my son's apparent resistance to figuring this out!

I assured this flustered mom that she wasn't failing, but that yes, eight was old enough for most kids to be able to get themselves ready. Sure, kids fall on a spectrum, but getting himself ready in the mornings wasn't an unrealistic expectation. I also let her know that there could be a lot more going on than what's on the surface. He could be intentionally resisting getting ready in the mornings. It might just be his way of getting attention from her. Kids are often lazy, although with stuff like this, most kids take pride in doing it themselves. I also told her there were echoes of my ADHD daughter in her son's story, so that might be something to consider and consult a professional about.

Regardless, there were basic skills she could be intentional about building in her son. Here were some simple things she could try:

- Teach him to set a wake-up alarm.
- Post lists of his morning routine in several places (bathroom, bedroom, kitchen, front door).
- Set a timer for each task to help him learn to pace himself and manage time.
- Teach him to prepare in advance by bathing and setting out his outfit the night before and having all his school stuff packed and at a launch pad by the door.

Teaching basic life skills is not a panacea guaranteed to reform your child's behavior. I can't get anyone in my family to consistently place their dirty socks in the hamper despite years of creative effort to teach this basic skill. Yet, just because it isn't always a quick-fix doesn't absolve us of the responsibility to teach. It's our job as parents. We have to teach basic skills, often over and over, and we must remember that our kids will all learn at different rates. I'm sure by the time my kids live in a house that they pay for, they'll have the sock-in-hamper skill figured out. If not, they're in their own place, so I don't have to care anymore.

Teach character traits

We not only need to instruct our children in basic skills, but we need to teach them the character traits of faith, integrity, endurance, courage, self-discipline, and poise. Always be on the lookout for teachable moments to instruct and demonstrate what the Bible says about things like kindness, love, hard work, honesty, trust, balance, and sacrifice.

One time I spoke to a women's group about building character, and a mom came up to me wanting to know how to help her daughter. She said her fourth grader tends to start a project and then as soon as it becomes a little hard, she gives up. She has joined several sports teams and wants to quit after the first practice.

I told her it could be that her daughter was feeling crippled by perfectionism, but beyond that, maybe she could be intentional to build her daughter's endurance and teach her to hang in there when stuff gets hard. Here are some practical suggestions I made for her:

- Help her break hard tasks into smaller steps.
- Offer to stand alongside her when she gets to a point she wants to quit. Give her a shoulder rub, make her a hot chocolate she can drink while she works, or help her brainstorm solutions.
- Always cheer for her when she's doing hard things, even if they seem silly or insignificant.
- Reiterate that *finishing* is what excites you most about doing hard things, not winning or perfection.
- Anytime she finishes something hard, celebrate. Regardless of outcome, finishing is its own triumph.

Teaching character is a process. It's an ongoing task that never ends for us as parents . . . like laundry! Mostly, our kids will learn godly character by watching how we live. They will notice what spills out of us when we get shaken. Yet, we can still be on the lookout for life's dilemmas that provide us with great opportunities to talk about and practice godly character with our kids in real time.

Distract

Distraction is an underutilized but powerful tool to avoid or end unwanted behavior quickly. Once you master this, you'll wonder what you did without it. It requires anticipating potential problems, planning creative diversions in advance, and sometimes thinking on your feet to invent quick diversions on the fly. Here are some examples.

Plan distractions in advance

Travel is tough on kids. They get hungry, tired, uncomfortable, and totally off their routine. Preparing distractions in advance helps get through travel days with a smidge of sanity intact. Pack snacks, provide new dollar-store toys you reveal one by one throughout the day (I saw a mom on a plane who'd wrapped each new cheap toy for extra anticipation), bring airport games, download movies on tablets—anything to divert your kids' focus. Change up the distractions frequently so your kids don't get bored.

Create distraction on the fly

If your three-year-old is struggling at dinner with your out-of-town relatives and starting to act out, you could take her on a walk around the restaurant to name every green thing she sees. Or if you're pretty sure your four-year-old son is going to react to the other boy at the park playing with his big wheel, to avoid a scuffle, before he notices the big wheel, challenge him to a race around the oak tree and back.

Redirect

Just like my dog, Mabel, kids are incapable of doing nothing. If your kids are doing something you don't want them to do, especially if it's an ongoing problem, it might be time to redirect that negative energy and behavior toward an acceptable, positive alternative.

For example, your six-year-old, high-energy, strong-willed son often gets frustrated and tends to take out his frustration physically by hitting you, his sister, your antique lamp, anything within range. You consistently tag the behavior, correct him, and give consequences, but the behavior keeps happening. So on Saturday morning, you take him to the sporting goods store and have him help you pick out a punching bag. You set up the punching bag in a central part of the house and any time you see him getting ready to hit, you say, "Punching bag" to remind him to hit the bag instead.

Here are a couple more guidelines to help you ensure that your redirection is effective:

Practice the redirection at times when he's calm

Maybe ask him to remember times he got really mad and then have him punch the bag.

Teach your child to self-monitor

Let him know that he can go punch his bag anytime he feels the need. The goal is for kids to learn to self-monitor and choose the positive alternative instead.

Another example of redirection: *Bored* isn't a four letter word, but in my house we treat it like one. When one of my kids approaches me and whines that they're bored, first, I remind them that I am their mother, not their cruise director. It's not my job to keep them entertained. Use the "B" word within my earshot and you'll get a chore assigned immediately.

My kids are surrounded by entertainment, beauty, activities, toys, electronics, books, and animals. If they choose to take the lazy route by complaining, I will come up with a cure for their boredom, but not usually the cure they are hoping for. Assigning my kids a chore when they say they're bored isn't intended as retaliation, even though I usually have to do my mental basket exercise so I don't go full Hulk on them. No, I assign them a chore because I know that kids *can't do nothing*. I redirect their lazy, whiny, unimaginative slump toward something else. And you know what's kind of annoying? My kids usually end up having fun washing my car, scrubbing the baseboards, or pulling weeds. They end up enjoying their consequence. They seem at peace knowing what they should do instead of wallowing in their boredom.

Use Positive Reinforcement

Positive reinforcement is anything that gives your kid a reason to continue the behavior. This is sometimes called positive consequences.

Use positive reinforcement as a way to intentionally praise and reward *wanted* behavior. Just like negative consequences, the younger the child, the more immediate the praise, reward, or reinforcement needs to be. Older kids can understand long-term rewards or praise/reinforcement later in the day for something that happened in the past.

Beware that positive reinforcement can work against you when you aren't intentional about it. If your five-year-old is whining and you react (whether that's to give him what he's whining for or yelling at him or other negative attention), you might be reinforcing behavior you don't want.

Giving your kids advance notice about a positive reward they can earn (such as a treat or picking a movie at home) if they behave a certain way (like staying in the cart the entire time at the grocery store) helps them predict the outcome of their behavior and motivates them to choose good behavior.

Encourage

In grace-based discipline, encouragement is finding a strength to praise, even if that strength is being expressed in an illegitimate way.

My dad always says, "Our strengths, when pushed to an

extreme, become our greatest weaknesses." There are lots of times we can call out our kids' strengths, even while tagging inappropriate behavior and issuing consequences.

For example, a kid who tattles a lot might have a strong sense of justice and cares deeply that things are fair. You can say, "You're so good at noticing when things aren't fair and people aren't being treated equally. God is going to use that for good things—but right now, you're overdoing it and watching other people like a hawk so you can tattle on them. How would you feel if someone did that to you?"

Or maybe your twelve-year-old daughter is constantly argumentative. You can say, "Wow, you have such a sharp mind! I think buried deep in there is an awesome gift. Maybe God wants you to be a lawyer someday. Right now, though, you're making me your target and using a disrespectful tone. That won't get you anywhere with a judge . . . or with me!"

Give Do-Overs

Do-overs offer a chance to rewind and do something again. They're a powerful tool to allow kids the chance to say something a different way or with a different tone.

Do-overs can teach our kids that it's okay to share their thoughts, opinions, and concerns, but they need to do it in honoring and respectful ways. This takes practice, though, and our kids (and we) don't always get it right.

Do-overs help our kids practice phrasing hard topics in kind ways by forcing them to apply their knowledge to relevant situations. They are redemptive and help create a culture of forgiveness. And do-overs require kids to self-assess to determine what part of their behavior, words, or tone needs to be corrected. Kids tend to be most receptive to their assessments of their own behavior.

For example, your kid says, "Again, Mom?! I'm so sick of chicken!"

You say, "Stop, rewind, do-over."

Then your kid tries, "Wow, we've been eating lots of chicken! Can I make myself a PBJ instead?"

Here's another example. Your thirteen-year-old daughter comes home from school, slams the front door behind her, and throws her backpack across the room. You say, "Stop, rewind, go back outside, do-over."

She goes outside, comes back in the door, closes it normally, hangs her backpack on the hook, and rushes to you as she starts to cry. (She and her best friend had a fight.)

Sadness, hurt, and confusion can come out as anger, destructiveness, or violence. Do-overs give kids a chance to reassess what's really driving them, and then seek help and comfort for it.

Engineer Their Environment for Success

Grace-based discipline seeks to create environments and situations that set our kids up to behave in ways that are in their best interest. We can't do this all the time, and life doesn't always work out this way either, but grace-based parents try not to create environments that make it harder than it needs to be for their kids to do what they know is right. A two-year-old will have a hard time successfully behaving in a house full of breakable heirlooms. A Fun Country kid will wither in a rigid, hyperorganized environment. More than just the practical, physical environment, if we frequently put our kids in situations where they feel entrapped or backed into a moral dilemma, we set them up to fail.

When I think about engineering a child's environment for success, I remember an example of this from my own parents. I was nineteen, attending Arizona State University, and working several part-time jobs. I was also living in my parents' house at the time to save money for my own apartment. Even though at nineteen I was an adult, as part of living at home, the rule was that unless I was working (my job often had me leaving work after midnight) or was at a structured activity like a movie with friends that necessitated me being out later, my curfew was midnight. It was a house rule based in practicality more than anything else.

Mike and I were dating, and we were in that love-struck phase where all we wanted to do in every minute of our spare time was hang out together.

One fateful night, I completely lost track of time. I'd been over at Mike's place watching a movie. After it finished, his roommates, a few of my friends, and Mike and I launched into the world's most epic game of dominoes. Fueled by Jack in the Box tacos and Dr. Pepper, we played for hours. It was 3 a.m. before we knew it.

As soon as I realized the time, I said quick good-byes, got in my car, and hurried home. I parked in my usual spot in the driveway, closed my car door as quietly as possible, and made a stealthy reentry into the house. As far as I could tell, no one was awake. It seemed I had dodged a bullet.

I woke up the next morning at the crack of 11:27 and made my way downstairs to have a meal before heading to my afternoon classes. My dad was sitting at the table with his laptop and a disheveled-looking newspaper spread out next to him.

I gave him a wary side-eye as I tried to saunter nonchalantly to the cupboard for a cereal bowl.

"Karis, what time did you get home last night?" he asked.

I looked up and started to open my mouth to answer—but before I could get a word out, my dad continued. "Before you say anything, I should disclose a key piece of information that I'm privy to."

"Uh, yeah, what's that?" I said, starting to sweat.

"You parked on top of the newspaper."

I stared blankly at him.

He explained, "Your front driver's side tire was directly on top of it. I had to move your car to get the paper this morning."

It started to dawn on me what he was really saying.

"Since I often leave super early when I travel, I happen to know that our newspaper gets delivered around 3:15 a.m."

"Sounds about right," I said.

"So, now, what time did you get home last night?"

"3:20," I said.

"Thanks for telling the truth."

My dad didn't have to explain it; I knew why my being out so late affected the rest of the family. It wasn't that my parents didn't trust me or that they were trying to snuff out my social life with a lame-sauce midnight curfew. It's just that I was part of a big picture: a family, a home. I got that it was near impossible for fully engaged parents to go off-duty until all the chicks are back in the nest. Even though I was a mostly grown chick, my mom and dad couldn't really rest until I was home safely.[28]

You should also know that when I was nineteen, my youngest brother was only nine and my other two siblings were in junior high and high school. They had to get up for school and responsibilities early in the morning. No matter how late my parents were up waiting for me to come home, morning still came early. The rest of the family couldn't adopt my crazy collegiate sleeping schedule.

"Would you like to tell me why you came home at 3:20 without calling and checking in?" he asked.

---

28 During the months I lived in the college dorms and then later in my own apartment, this rule didn't apply because I was able to operate in a vacuum of independence, and my curfew didn't affect anyone but me.

"I can honestly say that dominoes made me do it."

"Pizza?"

"No, the game . . . with the dots." I told him about getting carried away playing Mexican Train with my friends.

There were plenty of instances where Mike and I had lingered too long in a post-date kiss or fallen asleep on his couch watching a movie that I would not have been eager to answer for, but this time, my reason for breaking curfew was an impromptu dominoes tournament. It was so ridiculously nerdy, it had to be true.

And my dad believed me. I'd rarely given him reason not to. Honesty is my default mode because my parents had worked hard to make integrity the culture of our home. They also weren't in the habit of backing us into moral corners where we felt we either had to lie or die. They were intentional to engineer a pathway for us to exercise character as often as possible.

That's what my dad did when he tipped me off to my newspaper parking job. He diffused a moment that could have compelled me to fudge the timeline of my arrival home. If he hadn't offered me an out, I might have lied and said I got home at a more *acceptably late* hour—say, 1:30 a.m. Instead, he intentionally shared some key evidence so that I could see that the safest exit from this sticky situation was the door labeled *Truth*.

Grace doesn't position itself like a detective trying to keep the perpetrator in the dark and entrap them in a web of lies. Grace doesn't manipulate the situation and misuse its power. No, grace is *completely transparent*. I don't know how long my dad thought about how he was going to confront me, but even if it was only for a split second, this pivotal few minutes proves that relationships defined by grace are ones where parents make every effort to engineer their kids' environment for success.

Shift Expectations

Sometimes we might even need to rethink a rule or shift an expectation (I'm not talking about moral or character issues here) so our kids can be successful more often than not. For example, I have a friend who found a creative way to permanently correct an ongoing problem they'd had little success solving with consequences.

I *promise* this is the last anecdote that will compare kids and dogs!

My friend's kids were three and four at the time. Between the two of them, they were coming into bed with him and his wife, being carried back to their own beds, then returning several times a night. No one was getting more than fifteen minutes of sleep in a row, and the parents usually had someone's toe up their nose during those minutes. Everyone was miserable. They'd tried all the stuff their doctor recommended. They'd tried to implement the advice in sleep training books, but it continued for months and everyone had reached their breaking point. They were dealing with so many other behavioral issues with their kids that they had no strength to discipline because they were spent.

My friend was at the store one Saturday when in a moment of brilliance and clarity, he decided to buy a giant dog bed. He had the breakthrough thought that maybe if they all just slept a little, the landscape of their battlefield might look different.

He brought the giant dog bed home and made a big deal about how this was his kids' "special bed" in Mommy and Daddy's room. Mommy and Daddy weren't allowed to sleep in the kids' special bed, but the kids weren't allowed to sleep in Mommy and Daddy's bed either. He wanted everyone to do their best to sleep in their own bedrooms all night, but if they had to, they could come in to Mommy and Daddy's room and sleep in their special bed if they promised not to wake up Mom or Dad.

Everyone agreed to the terms, so they set up the kids' special bed on the floor next to the parents' bed. Some nights the kids stayed in their beds. Often, my friend and his wife would wake in the morning to find one or both kids sleeping in their special bed. It wasn't perfect, but the vast majority of nights, everyone respected the terms. The kids had something acceptable they could do instead of waking Mom and Dad at night but could still feel the comfort of being close to them.

Also, the kids were able to listen and behave better during the day because they were rested. Mom and Dad were able to deal with the disciplinary landscape of their home better, too, because they weren't angry zombies anymore.

His creative solution worked for them.

And the kids grew up. No one makes dog beds big enough for their fourteen-year-old daughter and fifteen-year-old son, and they don't need them anyway. Now, my friends are at a stage in life where they might love to go back, *just for one night*, to the time their kids snuck into bed to cuddle with them.

A Final Question

Once you've implemented your multipronged strategy for grace-based discipline and you've formulated whatever response you think is warranted to your kids' behavior, there's one last question you can ask yourself that, for me, has always been fail-safe.

Is this the way that God parents me?

If you're still unsure how to respond to your kids' defiance, ask, "How does God respond to me?"

If you're still unclear about what to do about your kids' behavior, ask, "How does God discipline me?"

Here's the thing: *our homes are laboratories for the gospel.* How we parent, and how we discipline, will be evidence that will either support or disprove whether the gospel is the good news we all claim. Our kids will know that grace works as they see it work in us. They will trust that the gospel transforms if they watch it transform us.

More than anything, we've got to get out of our own way and let God parent our children through us. That's how faith will come alive in our kids.

A CLEARER PICTURE OF GOD

Most of my life I've had nearly perfect eyesight. I've also largely taken it for granted.

A while back, I started getting bad headaches at the end of most days. At night, especially while driving, I had a harder time with depth perception and I noticed that light seemed streaky in my peripheral vision.

I went for an eye exam since it'd been a few years. (Okay, it had been *six years* when I looked at my medical file. Kids are why we can't have nice things, like brain cells, anymore.)

I went to one of those retail centers where you can get your eyes examined and your frames and eyeglass prescription filled at the same time. A technician used a series of machines to test my eyes. (Raise your hand if you want to vote the "puff test machine" off the island.)

After the technician used the thingamajigs, the doctor brought me into a room with the lab results, put a series of lenses in front of my eyes, and asked me, "Which is clearer? This? Or that?" Somehow, based on my answers, the doctor wrote me a prescription.

All I'd ever needed before were weak reading glasses. The prescription this doctor wrote was *wildly* different than anything I'd ever been prescribed. She wanted to correct for both near- and farsightedness as well as astigmatism, a diagnosis no other eye doctor had ever given me. Also, I'd have to wear these glasses *all the time*. Like a grown-up!

I wanted another opinion. In the course of a month, I went for two more eye exams. Each doctor's prescription was different.

One told me I needed only reading glasses to correct my far-sightedness (even though he said I'm both near- and farsighted) because he felt reading and using the computer were causing my eyes the most strain. The other wanted to correct both my near and farsightedness with bifocals. Neither doctor said anything about astigmatism.

I was starting to feel as if they were just *guessing*.

It was time to enlist a friend who had been an optician. I brought my exam charts to her one afternoon and supervised our kids in the backyard while she looked over everything.

I asked her to use small words to explain to me what was going on. She said different types of eye doctors use different ways of notating prescriptions, like different languages. But even once she'd translated and compared them, there was still a significant difference in the prescriptions each doctor wrote. What *were* consistent were my lab results. All three labs measured my near- and farsightedness as nearly identical. All three labs showed me as having astigmatism.

"So why the different prescriptions?" I said.

"Well," she said, "measuring people's eyes and diagnosing vision deficiencies has gotten very precise with modern diagnostic tools and technology, but *prescribing* isn't an exact science. It relies on the doctor's clinical experience, instincts, and the way you respond to his 'this or that' questions when he tries out lenses on you."

This wasn't building my confidence in the process. "So three different doctors had basically the same information about my eyes, but they all took a different approach to correcting my vision?"

"That's the 'practicing' part of the term 'practicing medicine,'" she quipped.

"Which prescription should I go with?" I asked.

"Just pick the doctor you felt best about, fill the prescription, and see how you like your glasses after a few weeks. With a good prescription, you'll see well enough that you won't think about your vision anymore."

"So, I'm not going to achieve perfection here?"

"Nope. We can't *perfectly* correct vision with artificial lenses, but we can get close enough that the distortion doesn't distract you anymore . . . at least not while you're wearing your glasses."

Imperfect Lenses

As parents, we are the first lenses through which our kids see God.

The way we parent our kids can have a profound impact on how they view God. As my friend said, prescribing isn't an exact science and different parents will have different approaches, but the ideal is that we don't create a distracting amount of distortion in how our kids see God, and the best way we know how to do that is by parenting our kids the way God parents us.

Parenting (and disciplining) our kids the way God does requires that we see our Father for who He really is. It's hard to copy a picture you can't see.

Unfortunately, the way many parents were parented themselves gave them a distorted view of God. None of us has perfect parents, though in my opinion mine are the best, and many of you might say the same of yours. But if your parents were misguided in their approach, or worse, absent, abusive, or neglectful in their treatment of you, it's tainted the bonds between you that are supposed to be a representation of God's love.

That's why it's good news that no matter what kind of lenses your earthly parents are (even if they're amazing), and no matter how distorted our kids' lenses are (that's us), *God is still the same.* How crisply we see Him or how distorted our view of Him is as a result of our lenses hasn't changed His character; it's only affected how we see.

God loved you before the world was formed, and the fact that He still loves you after all you've done might seem unbelievable based on the impression you got from your own parents. That you are offered the full measure of God's favor and His grace regardless of what you do or don't do might seem all but insane based on distorted lenses and what we know of our human capacity for love and forgiveness.

We are image-bearers of God, which is why we have any capacity for love and forgiveness, but we eventually come up against our own limitations. Yet God's love, favor, kindness, forgiveness, holiness, knowledge, and grace have no limits.

The best news as children of earthly parents, and now as parents ourselves, is that God's love covers a multitude of mistakes (1 Peter 4:8), whether those mistakes are our parents', our kids', or our own.

If we will accept it, God's grace serves as the self-healing mechanism for our inadequate lenses when we fail at love, forgiveness, and grace itself. His grace can make us into good-enough lenses:

- When we remind ourselves that our kids are uniquely created by God, that even though they're (sometimes adorable) little sinners, they're also unconditionally loved and favored by God . . .
- When we realize that God is not a cosmic scorekeeper but that Jesus settled the score on the cross . . .
- When we comprehend that sin has already been punished and paid for on the cross and God isn't trying to get even

with us when we sin but offers grace-based discipline that is for our good . . .

- When we remember God loves us and our kids exactly as we are, but He also loves us too much to let us stay that way . . .
- When we understand that we were, and still are, children just like our kids and even the best earthly parents pale in comparison to our heavenly Father . . .

. . . then we'll have a clearer picture of who God has always been. That helps us become the best possible lens through which our kids see God. It helps our kids focus more on their hope and forget about their artificial, imperfect, but hopefully good-enough lenses.

In case you're wondering, I went with the first doctor's prescription. I have bifocals that correct for astigmatism. I even have a pair of sunglasses too. I have to act like a big girl and wear them all the time.

I'm back to taking my good vision for granted.

Paint the Fence

If you started reading this book as someone well versed in the philosophy and strategies of grace-based parenting, if the theology of parenting is deeply imbedded in your family's current culture, then you've started off on third base. You've already been investing the raw materials in your kids that will give them the ability to become adults who live transformed lives for Christ.

You may have started out with a little headway. I suspect, though, that you're here because you wanted to learn even more ways to apply grace while you're in the daily trenches of discipline with your kids.

When our kids are at their worst, responding with grace-based discipline, rather than a panicked reaction, requires an intentional consciousness built upon correct ideological foundations. But even with that, some folks still struggle to build from there.

Just remember, grace-based parenting is, and has always been, a comprehensive plan for discipline.

My goal has merely been to deliver those life-changing truths to you in a new way. Sometimes transformation happens because minds are enlightened, paradigms are shifted, and then actions change.

Just as often—and this might be the quieter revolution you find yourself in—transformation happens because actions change, outcomes challenge assumed paradigms, and then minds are enlightened and changed.

The good news is, even if you'd never heard of grace-based parenting prior to reading this book, you've learned its philosophy, in real time, by doing. By implementing the strategies and tactics explained in this book, you are internalizing the philosophy of grace-based parenting by default.

Like the Karate Kid, you're mastering an ancient martial art (grace-based parenting) and painting the fence at the same time (grace-based discipline). You're happy. Your kids are happy. Mr. Miyagi is happy.

The Prize

All the years we spend responding to our kids with gracious, loving correction and forging a relationship that echoes the communion we have with our heavenly Father add up to a rich investment in people who will affect a world we will likely never see.

At the park I watched a landscaper stand by the sidewalk and use his leaf blower to blow water off the concrete while the sprinklers ran. He did this for the full fifteen-minute irrigation cycle. The sprinklers spewed water on the sidewalk, and the landscaper diligently removed it. The artificial rain kept coming, and he kept blowing it off.

I was fascinated because I couldn't understand the point. If he just walked away and did something else, waited out the sprinklers, I'm not sure any harm would have befallen the sidewalk. Last time I checked, concrete was pretty good at repelling water. I'm not sure what goal he was trying to accomplish or what calamity he was trying to prevent.

In the thick of parenting, we can feel like a landscaper blowing an endless stream of water off a concrete sidewalk. We feel crazy, and I'm pretty sure we look crazy to any observer whose bewildered attention we've drawn.

Also, discipline sometimes feels futile. It feels as though it isn't making a difference. What's the point of blowing off all the water if it's just going to keep coming?

In the case of the landscaper at the park, I have no idea.

But in your case, weary parent, if you feel your discipline is pointless, I say, carry on. Keep responding with grace. Your efforts might feel futile now, but they're not.

The payoff is that in the not-so-distant future your children will become an asset to the world around them. Kids parented with grace have a tendency to be others-oriented and focused on the things in life that have eternal value. With careful, grace-based discipline, our kids' differences, especially the ones that got on your nerves, blossom into gifts they use to serve the world.

When we stay in the crazy-hard race of parenting, when we run and love with all our hearts, when we finally come over the last hill and have the finish line in sight, that's when we'll see our prize standing just on the other side.

Can you see your prize? Can you see your reward? Can you see the faces of your children?

I can see mine too. Our kids are our prize. Raising kids who grow up to be adults who love a hurting world and transform it for God's glory is all the reward we need. They are worth every drop of sweat, every strain, every tear, and every second of lost sleep.

We're worth everything to God. Our kids are worth everything to us.

FOUR TRUTHS FOR PARENTING IN THE DIGITAL AGE[29]

Parenting has always been tough. But technology, social media, and the virtual space have added nuance and complexity to the job of raising kids. Our generation, born in the 1970s and '80s, had front-row seats to the rise of the digital age. We're probably the only generation who has actually used both a card catalog and a networked computer to do research at our school library.

Our kids, on the other hand, are born with code in their blood. If you need proof, just watch a baby play with a smartphone or tablet. Our kids now hold in the palms of their hands some of the most powerful, elegant, and intuitive computers ever built.

Right now, we're at a threshold where technology is a second language to parents but a native tongue to their kids. Even the most tech-savvy of us often feel we're at a disadvantage to monitor, protect, and guide our kids through the minefield that is the Internet.

With every new software, model, mode, and media, we feel we need fresh, nuanced instructions for how to parent. Every time a new social media outlet dawns, it raises the battle cry from vigilant moms and dads. We should, by all means, stay informed,

---

29 This appendix is an article by Karis Murray, originally written for the Family Matters Blog, entitled, "4 Truths for Parenting in the Digital Age," Family Matters (blog), October 20, 2015. http://fmlymtt.rs/4digtaltruths.

involved, and vigilant. Yet I know many parents simply withdraw because they feel like their parenting strategies are always chasing a constantly changing threat.

Does it help to know that ancient wisdom still applies? Does it ease your mind to know that human beings really haven't changed that much? God's Word stayed true through the Renaissance, the Industrial Revolution, and the World Wars. God's Word remains true in the Digital Age.

We don't need a special instruction manual to parent in the Digital Age. We just need grace, truth, and the Holy Spirit.

#1: Behind Every Profile, Avatar, Post, and Program Is a Real Person Whom Jesus Loves

God's Word teaches that the Great Commandment is to "Love the Lord your God with all your heart and with all your soul and with all your strength and with all your mind, and your neighbor as yourself" (Luke 10:27).

Our job as Christian parents is to do our best to live out our faith by loving God and loving people and to raise our kids to treat others the way God treats them. We expect our kids to treat everyone online with the same standards of kindness, respect, and grace as they do face-to-face.

It also follows that because we are dealing with real people online, they are going to fall into a spectrum of beliefs, backgrounds, values, and behavior. We shouldn't assume that everyone will treat us with the same kindness, respect, and grace, but even that shouldn't change how *we* act. Yet teaching our kids to set and enforce boundaries and to know that not everyone is a "safe person" encourages them to "be wise as serpents and innocent as doves" (Matthew 10:16).

#2: You Are Never Anonymous Online

Evil, unkindness, and stupidity thrive in the darkness. People can do awful things when they think they're invisible. We can hide for a while behind firewalls and proxy IPs, but if someone is looking, they can always find us. We teach our kids this principle because it's the digital iteration of "be sure your sin will find you out" (Numbers 32:23). The reality that you are never truly anonymous online provides accountability, and we all benefit from a little more of that.

#3: Data Lives Forever

"Delete" is a myth. Nothing we do online is ever truly erased. There is a record of everything we do, post, send, and say on the Internet . . . *especially photos!* And, now that nearly every device we use is wirelessly connected to the Cloud, if we use a device to take a photo or video, or to create content, we must assume that it is now part of that eternal data, and we can't ever take it back. All of this data follows us forever and can be accessed by anyone who wants to know who we truly are . . . such as future employers and spouses!

We all make mistakes, both small and serious. The Internet never erases our sins, but fortunately for all of us, Jesus does. With repentance, God casts their sins "as far as the east is from the west" (Psalm 103:12).

#4: Character Matters Online Just Like Everywhere Else

Who our kids are online is only an extension of who they are at their core. Now more than ever, digital relationships are real relationships. Our kids' digital life *is* their real life. There's very little distinction between the two realms. Our kids' default programs should be *faith, integrity, poise, disciplines, endurance,* and *courage*. When we build character into our kids' hearts, we are installing the tools they will need to live a moral life whether the dilemmas they face exist in the physical or digital world.

None of these new challenges has caught God by surprise. He promises to equip us for every good deed (2 Timothy 3:17), which includes preparing our children not only to survive but to thrive in the digital age. For more on building the character traits of faith, integrity, poise, disciplines, endurance, and courage into your children, check out the book *Raising Kids Who Turn Out Right*.[30]

30   Tim Kimmel, *Raising Kids Who Turn Out Right* (Scottsdale, AZ: Family Matters, 2006).

TO SPANK OR NOT TO SPANK?

In order not to detract and derail our discussion about grace-based discipline tools and tactics, my section about spanking is a supplement. In this appendix, I will do my best to communicate clearly about spanking.

The Part Where I Talk About Spanking and Tick Everyone Off

To spank or not to spank? That is the question. When I speak to groups about discipline and even in the research panels I assembled in preparation to write this book, discussions about discipline always seem to boil down to whether or not to spank. The conversation always goes there, and it goes there fast. It's a line we've drawn in the sand, and there are two camps. We all want to know which side of the line the person we're talking to or listening to falls. If it's not the same side as we choose, we feel we can disregard everything that person says. We've put a microscope on the question of spanking and defined entire parenting methodologies around it. Heck, we've crafted complete movements around it.

That's why what I'm about to say might alienate everyone. Lucky me.

"Karis, what do you think about spanking? Should parents spank their kids or not?"

Answer: I don't care.

Spanking is *one small piece* of discipline. It is *one* legitimate tool among many you have available in your discipline toolbox.

You might *never* need to use the tool of spanking for your particular child. You may choose not to spank, for any number of legitimate reasons, in your particular context.

Or you might.

If you're a grace-based parent raising your kids in a grace-based culture, whether you choose to spank or not is up to you and *I don't care.*

I'll tell you a few things I do care about, though.

Abuse

I care about the abused and I care about the abusers. Child abuse happens, it's awful, it grieves the Lord, and it's a crime. Maybe it has happened to you. Maybe it's part of your past or part of your child's past. (I know this can be especially true for my friends whose kids came to their families through adoption or foster care.) If abuse is part of your family story, spanking might be a tool you choose to toss out. Maybe it just looks too similar to weapons that were used against you or your child.

But remember a knife can be used to make a death-blow to the heart or for life-saving heart surgery. It matters whose hands it's in. Not all spanking is abuse, and not all abuse is spanking.

I know for a fact that in the context of a grace-based home, within the boundaries of a loving heart connection between parent and child, when a parent is making a sacrificial choice to cause their child and themselves a little bit of pain now to protect them from a whole lot more pain later, abuse via spanking is not possible. Outside that context, all bets are off.

I've spent most of this book trying to ensure you understand

and implement a grace-based atmosphere in your home. If you have done so, you've forged the type of loving heart connections with your kids that will safeguard against abuse.

Focus on creating a culture of grace, setting fair rules and boundaries that exist for your child's best interest (rather than legislating your own convenience and preference), engineering their environment for success, redirecting their behavior toward acceptable options, and making discipline about your kids and not about you. You should be able to rate yourself 7 out of 10 or better in all those categories before you choose to spank. Until then, you won't be spanking, because what you are doing when you strike your child is not spanking, by definition. If you aren't acting within the context I've spent the entire book establishing *more often than you're not* (that's 7 out of 10), then striking your child is corporal punishment, not spanking. Corporal punishment and grace-based spanking are in different categories. There is no equivalency between the two.

Grace-based parents *never punish.* They only discipline.

If you now realize you've made some poor choices in the area of spanking, don't get caught in shame. Ask God and your kids for forgiveness as many times as necessary, in real time and retroactively, and then move forward and try to do better.

Neglect

Another thing I care about is neglect. This is the other extreme of the spanking/anti-spanking debate. Too often, when parents are vehemently anti-spanking, what they *actually are* is anti-discipline. For whatever reason, they say they don't believe in spanking, but really they simply don't want to discipline. Maybe they're lazy. Maybe they're afraid to the point they can't gather the will, out of love for their kid, to overcome it. Maybe they'd rather their kid like them in the moment than do what's best for their child in the long run. Ultimately, though, if your kid's leg is broken but you refuse to take him to the doctor and have it set (an act that you know will be profoundly painful), you are neglecting the best interest of your child—and that's worse.

Sending kids who don't know how to respect boundaries and have no regard for rules and standards out into a world with no tolerance for that type of behavior isn't loving or gracious. It's actually cruel. It's cruel because it subjects them to the unforgiving justice of society's court and nature's tribunal. Both society and nature are blind, swift, often harsh judges, juries, and executioners.

Advice for Those Who Spank

If you choose to spank, here is some advice to keep in mind as you carefully and prayerfully apply this discipline tool:

- *Spanking is a tool best fit for very young kids* because it's in line with their brain development. It allows for a swift, straightforward consequence that can be easily connected to an undesirable behavior. It requires no language or deductive reasoning skills. It utilizes our primal understanding of pain-avoidance to shape behavior.

- *I use my hand to spank.* I know there are those who recommend using an object (like a wooden spoon or paddle) so your child won't associate your hand with only spanking. I believe kids, even very young ones, are smarter than this. (I use my hands to feed them, hold them, wipe their noses and bottoms, and wash their hair. When I reach out for them, they don't assume a shampoo is coming.) You can use an object if you want to, but here's why I don't: I'm five foot ten and strong. An object in my hand multiplies my natural strength more than I'm comfortable with. It also disconnects me from experiencing physical pain *with* my child. When I spank with my hand, *I feel it too.* This, again, regulates the amount of force I use.

- *Do not spank in anger.* The adrenaline of anger makes us too strong when we spank. It also tempts us to punish, to retaliate, rather than discipline out of love. Send a child to their room, make them wait till you're calm, then come in and administer the spanking like a cop writes a speeding ticket. Cops aren't mad at you for speeding. They don't take personal offense. They just write the ticket.

- *The younger the child, the more immediate the consequence needs to be.* Young brains simply haven't developed the ability to connect a consequence to something that happened too far in the past. So if spanking is the tool you're using, and your child is two, you need a way to get your emotions in check almost immediately, so you can spank (or whatever else) almost immediately. Practice your imaginary mental basket exercise.

- *There should be no humiliation coupled with spanking.* Shame is not gracious. God never uses shame. For me, this means I'm pretty careful about spanking publicly or in the presence of anyone my kids would be embarrassed to have witness their spanking. Also, I never ask my kids to pull down their pants. That's just a "nope" in my book.

- *I spank bottoms only.* Sometimes I miss and strike upper legs, but that's never my intention. For very young toddlers, perhaps a swat on the top of their hand is okay. For the very young, your goal isn't to make it hurt so much as get their attention. The shock value hurts more than the actual swat. I remember that my strong-willed, high-energy toddlers could fall headfirst off the playground into the wood chips, stand up, say, "Ta-da," and keep on playing. Falling on their head had to hurt more than my swat on their hand or bottom, but they cried for a swat because it got their attention.

- *Any physical discipline that causes permanent physical harm is not a legitimate form of grace-based discipline.* You might say, "Duh," but you know I have to say it. A swat on their bottom or the top of their hand doesn't cause lasting physical harm. If it does, it was done in anger or with an object or with too much force. I've already warned you about those things, *and this is why.* Any other form of corporal punishment,[31] such as confinement in a small place, forcing kids to stand on one foot, to hold a heavy object a long time, to stand out in the cold or heat, to swallow soap or hot sauce . . . any of these have potential to cause lasting physical harm, and they're completely unnecessary. They also disconnect the parent from entering into the physical pain with their child, which I believe to be an important safeguard between using pain to punish, and retaliate, versus to discipline out of love.

- *There's rarely a reason to spank a kid older than about five.* After that age, you have many other developmentally appropriate and effective tools for discipline. A grace-based parent who chooses to spank does so only as often, and for only as long, as absolutely necessary. An older child is far more likely to be embarrassed by a spanking, which violates the shame/humiliation boundary. Also, it might not be as effective for an older child. When I was eleven, I'd much

---

31 I use the term "punishment" here intentionally. If it causes permanent harm, it is punishment, not discipline. Remember, grace-based parents never punish. Remember that all forms of corporal punishment and grace-based spanking are in completely different categories.

prefer getting a swift spanking that didn't hurt all that bad (but that option had been removed from my parents' arsenal many years earlier) than lose the privilege of going to my friend's house. For older kids, minor physical pain is not their main currency, and therefore it is not the currency in which discipline is most effectively administered.

As you'll see, my list of advice for parents who choose to spank is significantly longer than for those who don't. That's the way it *must* be. Spanking is a legitimate discipline tool, but it's a sharp one. It carries with it inherent risks and requires a level of caution and precision that other tools don't. Those of us who use it (and I did) have a higher level of accountability. We have greater responsibility to use spanking cautiously and sparingly.

Advice for Those Who Do Not Spank

If you choose not to spank, here is some advice as you select other tools from your discipline toolbox.

- *You have to do something else instead.* If your kids' behavior requires correction and consequences, disavowing spanking is not a license to disengage from discipline. There are still battles you must fight. You don't get to be Switzerland.
- *Pick alternative discipline tools.* If you choose not to spank, choose other grace-based discipline tools that are appropriate and effective, and use them consistently and predictably.
- *Decide which forms of pain you will use instead.* If you're choosing, for whatever reason (and there are plenty of legitimate ones), to swear off physical pain as a tool for loving discipline, then you must make your peace with using different types of pain instead (such as emotional pain caused by a consequence like a lost privilege). Remember that pain is necessary for

correction. You cannot discipline without it. Pain plays a loving role in discipline, and it has its rightful place. Just because pain often plays a vengeful, retaliatory, and damaging role in punishment *doesn't mean we outlaw the use of pain.* After all, God uses pain to discipline us. If you disagree, your argument is not with me; it's with Him.[32]

A New Camp

It turns out many parents drew and focused on the wrong line in the sand. We drew our dividing line between the spanking camp and the anti-spanking camp and stood glowering at each other from either side.

This has been the wrong perspective all along. There's a new camp. There's a radical and inclusive new movement. There's grace. And in the grace camp there are loving parents standing on either side of the spanking/anti-spanking line. We've been caught in a stare-down of condemnation against each other—and it turns out we've been brethren all along.

There are spankers who abuse their kids . . . *they are not our people.*

There are anti-spankers who neglect to discipline and therefore abuse by default . . . *they are not living in the grace camp.*

Let's stop focusing on the spanking/anti-spanking line we've drawn within the grace camp, look up, and notice the folks outside our walls who really need our help. Let's put our effort behind protecting wounded/abused/neglected children from their often also wounded/abusive/neglectful parents. While we're protecting those kids, let's pursue help, healing, and restoration for their parents. Let's preach to them the gospel of redemption that we know. We are the good news people, after all, and our lives won't preach if we're stuck in a spitting match against one another.

---

32 Hebrews 12:11; Proverbs 13:24; Proverbs 22:15.

If you're reading this, and you now realize you're outside the grace camp, you're welcome here. Our gates are never locked. All you have to do is repent and then walk in. We'll save a place for you around the campfire.

Jesus forgives, but there might be a price to pay for your actions here on earth.

If you've abused your kids with corporal punishment, we'll introduce you to our brethren who have chosen not to use spanking as a tool. For the rest of your life, you belong with them. We'll also require you to seek treatment from a team of people who can help heal you.[33] We might still need to protect your kids from you, which nearly always means involving the authorities, but know that it's in love—love for you, love for your kids, and love for Jesus.

If you've neglected your kids, if you've ignored their need for discipline, we'll introduce you to our brethren who can help you make your peace with pain so you can begin to accept its role in discipline. We'll hold you accountable to do the hard work, face the tough things, and enter into pain yourself so you can give your children the treatment they so desperately need: *grace-based discipline.*

---

33 People who abuse (in the context of corporal punishment, we're talking about physical violence) need professional treatment to get better. Pastors are important support staff in this case, but they are not enough. Someone who has abused a child (or a spouse, or anyone) will do it again without proper, intensive, long-term therapeutic treatment. Abusers have relational cancer, and pastors are not relational oncologists. An adult who routinely loses control of their violent impulses has a broken brain. Also, because actions and choices have consequences, we have a legal and moral obligation to report any knowledge of abuse of a child to the proper legal authorities. Failing to report any suspected abuse enables oppressors, withholds kindness and protection from the vulnerable, and is almost always a crime. If you know of abuse (any type, especially sexual or physical) or if you even suspect it, you report it to the police and you do it now. Reporting abuse to the proper legal authorities is not step 3, it's step 1.

About the Author

Karis Kimmel Murray is the oldest daughter of Christian relationship expert and bestselling, award-winning author Dr. Tim Kimmel. Karis grew up in the family that was the proving ground for the philosophy that turned traditional Christian parenting advice on its head. Her parents' radical message has helped transform relationships in tens of thousands of Christian families through her father's book, *Grace Based Parenting®*, as well as the Grace-Based Parenting ™ and Grace-Filled Marriage training events and video studies.

As the Creative Director for Family Matters® (the ministry behind the "grace message") Karis writes and speaks to a growing global audience to testify to the powerful influence grace-based parenting had on her upbringing, and as a parent now herself, why she and her husband are raising their daughters the same way.

With conversational style and humor, Karis connects with her readers and audiences on a heart level and swaps stories of trial and triumph . . . straight from the trenches of parenting.

Karis and her husband, Mike, reside in Scottsdale, Arizona, with their two teenage daughters and a growing menagerie of pets currently including two dogs, two cats, eleven chickens, a beta fish, and two hermit crabs.

If you enjoyed this book, read
the book that started it all . . .

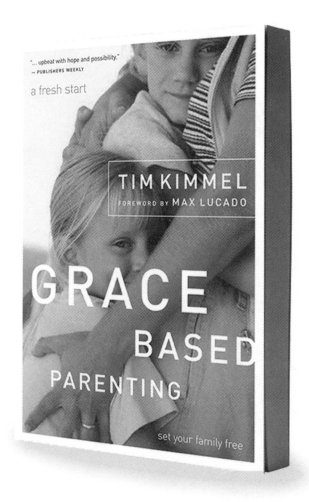

"Raise your kids the way
God raises His...with grace."
— Dr. Tim Kimmel

Visit:

gracebaseddiscipline.com

**For Study Guides,
News,
and More Information**